T0194805

ReCoVery

Re—Rebuild

Co—Together

Very—In Truth

The Spirit Of The Lord Is Upon Me, He Hath Anointed Me
To Share
The Message Of The Good News
To The Brokenhearted and Proclaim
ReCoVery
Of Sight To The Blind

Joy-Michael Bowser, D.Th. (R)

WESTBOW
PRESS®
A DIVISION OF THOMAS NELSON
& ZONDERVAN

This book is a work of non-fiction. Unless otherwise noted, the author and the publisher make no explicit guarantees as to the accuracy of the information contained in this book and in some cases, names of people and places have been altered to protect their privacy.

WestBow Press books may be ordered through booksellers or by contacting:

WestBow Press
A Division of Thomas Nelson & Zondervan
1663 Liberty Drive
Bloomington, IN 47403
www.westbowpress.com
844-714-3454

ISBN: 978-1-6642-5820-4 (sc)
ISBN: 978-1-6642-5821-1 (hc)
ISBN: 978-1-6642-5822-8 (e)

Library of Congress Control Number: 2022903174

Print information available on the last page.

WestBow Press rev. date: 08/18/2022

~*~ **DEDICATION** ~*~

TO MY

Father and Mother,

Oscar Bowser & Ireather Green Bowser

THE COMMISSION

1~ _He is with me_: The Spirit of the Lord is upon me

2~ _He has prepared me for the work_: Anointed me with His Glory

3~ _Christ's Intervention_: Preach the Gospel Good News

~JESUS~

4~ _Christ's Interventions is for_: The Broken & Blind Heart without Jesus

5~ _He Commissioned the work_: He sent Me and You

The Work

6~ Heal the Brokenhearted

7~ Preach Deliverance to the Captives

8~ _ReCoVery_ of sight to the Blind Hearted

9~ To set at Liberty them that are Bruised

The Results of the Work

10~ Freedom in Christ Jesus

Contents

Part 5   Forever

⹌*⹌ FOREWORD ⹌*⹌

This book was designed for anyone who wishes to get a grip, get on track, or move ahead. It is written to help you improve your health, happiness, and well-being. You do not have to be clinically diagnosed with a mental or physical disorder to find encouragement between the pages you are about to read. It can help you even if you've never experienced symptoms of addiction or problems related to alcohol or drug abuse. Although it is written for individuals seeking ReCoVery from life controlling issues. The scripture references, worksheets, and questionnaires can benefit anyone striving to live a life of victory.

Likewise, friends, family members, and caregivers of people in transition can use this to better understand the challenges of rising, after being knocked down. They can develop goals for supporting their loved one, learn how to provide a safe environment, and help their loved one stay motivated.

These writings do not propose to provide a quick fix or magical cure for all of life's challenges. It does not offer a simple solution to life's problems because maintaining focus and momentum is not easy. To get the most out of this guide, you will need to think about the words you read, determine how the information applies to you, and create strategies for implementing the tips and techniques in your daily life.

My Friend and Colleague

Joy⹌Michael Bowser

Has dedicated time before the Lord in prayer and supplication. Heaven heard her plea and poured out of her a message of relief for our souls. Read on and be Blessed - On Purpose!

Humbly in His Service

Reverend Winston
Cornelius Trumpet
Dean of Men at Brooklyn Adult & Teen Challenge Center
The Brooklyn Teen Challenge Recovery Ministry
Originally Founded by Reverend David WilkersonTime
Square Church New York, New York
Chief Executive Officer and Founder of Winston C. Trumpet & Associates, LLC
Executive Coaches & Consultants for Leaders of Nonprofit & Faith-Based Organizations
At Strategic Business Associates, LLC
Business Growth Consultant for Nonprofits & Faith-Based Organizations

~*~ **ACKNOWLEDGEMENT** ~*~

MY HEAVENLY FATHER
ABBA
MY
ALL IN ALL

"Blessed are You, Lord God of Israel, Our Father, Forever and Ever.
Yours, O Lord, is the Greatness, The Power and The Glory, The Victory and The Majesty
For All that is in Heaven and in Earth is Yours
Yours is the Kingdom
O Lord and You are Exalted as Head over All
Both Riches and Honor come from You
And
You Reign over All
In Your hand is Power and Might
In Your hand it is to make Great
And to
Give Strength to All"

—1 Chronicle 29:10–12 (NKJV)

This BOOK is a Declaration to

"ALL" who have sincerely said…

I'm Tired

I'm Tired

I'm Tired

I am Tired

I am Tired

I am Tired

I am Tired

I am Tired

I am Tired

I am Tired

I am Tired

I am Tired

I am Tired

I am Tired

I am Tired

I am Tired!

ReCoVery

Introduction

We know that the law is spiritual; but I am unspiritual, sold as a slave to sin. I do not understand what I do. For what I want to do I do not do, but what I hate I do. And if I do what I do not want to do, I agree that the law is good. As it is, it is no longer I myself who do it, but it is sin living in me. For I know that good itself does not dwell in me, that is, in my sinful nature. For I have the desire to do what is good, but I cannot carry it out. For I do not do the good I want to do, but the evil I do not want to do—this I keep on doing. Now if I do what I do not want to do, it is no longer I who do it, but it is sin living in me that does it. So I find this law at work: Although I want to do good, evil is right there with me. For in my inner being I delight in God's law; but I see another law at work in me, waging war against the law of my mind and making me a prisoner of the law of sin at work within me. What a wretched man I am! Who will rescue me from this body that is subject to death? Thanks be to God, who delivers me through Jesus Christ our Lord! So then, I myself in my mind am a slave to God's law, but in my sinful nature a slave to the law of sin.

—Romans 7:14–25 (NIV)

ReCoVery

ReCoVery is traditionally associated with addictions. However, as I have engaged with life, I have found that "ReCoVery is truly a constant," a constant element of life. Individuals are involved in the ReCoVery process daily. When there is a need for ReCoVery, there has been a perception of loss. ReCoVery is a necessary factor associated with ongoing losses. We experience loss of family members, spouses, children, physiological health, psychological well-being, emotional stability, financial support, belongings, and security due to terrorist attacks on our beloved homeland in America and the world. These diverse losses are due to multiple situations, circumstances, and relationships in our lives. The losses will undoubtedly result in life stresses, strains, responsibilities, and fears. People are recovering from surgery, shame, guilt, assault, abuse, incest, theft in many areas of their lives, and a worldwide crisis. The entire world must go through one of the largest ReCoVery processes known for such a time as this, a world pandemic.

No one on earth has immunity to COVID-19 because no one has had this particular strain of COVID until 2019. The outcome of the COVID-19 pandemic is impossible to predict at the time of this writing. But we can learn from pandemics in history— the Spanish flu, the AIDS pandemic, and more—to determine our best course. Cholera, bubonic plague, smallpox, and influenza are some of the most brutal killers in human history. And outbreaks of these diseases across international borders are properly defined as a pandemic, especially smallpox, which throughout history has killed between 300 to 500 million people in its 12,000-year existence.[1]

The answers to ReCoVery are question-driven: Are you ready to recover? Are you going to fight to regain your losses, or are you just dreaming of recovering? Are you ready to recover from diseases, sicknesses, and addiction? Are you ready to de-thrall your enthrallment? Recovery is a daily sequential fight. ReCoVery is obtainable based on an independent inner decision. The intensity of the desire to go through the process will depend on you, the person experiencing the loss.

In computers, one may lose a page if there is an abrupt closure. Upon reopening the document, the computer will ask, "Is there a need to recover the page?" When individuals divorce, a recovery process will take place for both individuals. What happens when an individual experiences a limb amputation? The ReCoVery process from the loss of an amputated part is a tremendously challenging situation. One will have to engage in physical therapy, get fitted for a prosthesis, and learn to utilize the prosthetic by going through tremendous emotional and physiological pain about the limb. An athlete must recover from their defeat. Hence, recovery is a constant in life for everyone at some point or another. It is a battle fighting for your life.

The battle is in the body, mind, and soul. Before ReCoVery can occur, we need a transformation of our minds, thoughts, and reasoning. We have choices in life all the time: to be victorious and conquer our fears or settle for defeat. We do have to pick our battles even when the battle belongs to the Lord.

To begin the ReCoVery process, these are some addressed issues as follows: I desire ReCoVery, I have hope in my ReCoVery, and I have faith in Jesus Christ to help me in my ReCoVery process. Faith is the propelling force that pushes one through the fear. We all fear new and

ReCoVery

old experiences on a day-to-day basis, but we cannot afford to remain stuck in the posture of fear because that is where you will remain, stuck. Fear will paralyze one in midstream because that is what it is designed to do, to keep one still motionless, lifeless, and noncommitted except to the fear. But all things are possible with Christ Jesus, including ReCoVery.

Matthew Henry reads from John 17,

> that Jesus Christ whom, thou have sent, as Mediator, doctrines, and laws of that holy religion which he instituted for the ReCoVery of man out of his lapsed state. Here is the origin of his power: Thou hast given him power; he has it from God, to whom all power belongs. Man, in his fallen state, must, in order to his ReCoVery, be taken under a new model of government, which could not be erected but by a special commission under the broad seal of heaven, directed to the undertaker of that glorious work, and constituting him sole arbitrator of the grand difference that was, and sole guarantee of the grand alliance that was to be, between God and man; so as to this office, he received his power, which was to be executed in a way distinct from his power and government as Creator.[2]

For some of us, our quest for ReCoVery is a discovery of self. Your lives can be taken from dysfunctional to functional lives. The transformation will allow you to function with full capacity of what you were designed and purposed to do as an individual, the purpose for which you were designed to exist with enjoyment.

ReCoVery

A Prayer For ReCoVery

I Desire ReCoVery:

- *ReCoVery to believe in ~ Jesus Christ and me*
- *ReCoVery to believe ~ Jesus Christ is my friend who is closer than my brother*
- *ReCoVery of a friendly relationship between ~ Jesus Christ and Me*
- *ReCoVery to accept ~ Jesus Christ as my Personal Savior*
- *ReCoVery to come to terms with ~ Jesus Christ directing my life*
- *ReCoVery of the cause to coexist in harmony with ~ Jesus Christ and Me*
- *ReCoVery to show to be compatible ~ I am made in the image of Jesus Christ.*
- *ReCoVery to Learn to live with ~ Jesus Christ*
- *ReCoVery to Learn to live in ~ Jesus Christ*
- *ReCoVery to Learn to live for ~ Jesus Christ*
- *ReCoVery to learn to fall in love with ~ Jesus Christ because He first loved me*
- *ReCoVery to love~ Living in a lifelong relational experience with Jesus Christ*
- *ReCoVery to learn to make ~ Jesus Christ My ~All in All*
- *ReCoVery to accept the undesired ~ Jesus Christ, whom I had not known of my first birth, nor did I naturally desire to know him. Now, since engaged in my born-again experience; I desire to learn of Him more and more.*

ReCoVery

Prelude

The Book of Romans

Romans is the sixth book of the New Testament. It was written by Paul, an apostle, appointed preacher, and teacher of the gospel of Jesus Christ to the Gentiles (i.e., non-Jewish people, you and me). It is also called the Pauline Epistles, or Letters of Paul.

Paul was truly an interested forerunner of the gospel. The Apostle Paul initially hated Christians. He persecuted them with a loving passion for killing them. But God, Christ Jesus, changed his life. The salvation of Jesus Christ transformed him. Paul informs us that he was indeed a man of status.

I am indeed a Jew, born in Tarsus of Cilicia, but brought up in this city at the feet of Gamaliel (Pharisee a teacher of the law, who was honored by all the people), taught according to the strictness of our fathers' law, and was zealous toward God as you all are today … So I said, "Lord, they know that in every synagogue I imprisoned and beat those who believe on You. And when the blood of Your martyr Stephen was shed, I also was standing by consenting to his death, and guarding the clothes of those who were killing him." (Acts 22:3, 19–20 NKJV)

In Paul's words,

I'm sure that you've heard the story of my earlier life when I lived in the Jewish way. In those days I went all out in persecuting God's church. I was systematically destroying it. I was so enthusiastic about the traditions of my ancestors that I advanced head and shoulders above my peers in my career. Even then God had designs on me. Why, when I was still in my mother's womb he chose and called me out of sheer generosity! Now he has intervened and revealed his Son to me so that I might joyfully tell non-Jews about him … Then I began my ministry in the regions of Syria and Cilicia. After all that time and activity, I was still unknown by face among the Christian churches in Judea. There was only this report: That man who once persecuted us is now preaching the very message he used to try to destroy. Their response was to recognize and worship God because of me! (Galatians 1:13–16, 21–24 MSG)

I was led to use the book of Romans as the pathway for this ReCoVery process. Throughout the book of Romans, the apostle Paul focuses on presenting the gospel of Jesus Christ by persuasion. He communicates the need for having the gospel in your life and the need to serve in the kingdom of God. Once accepting Jesus Christ as Lord and Savior, there is no need to look back on what was but press toward the mark of a future life. I believe that people often experience so much hurt and destruction in the past that they hold on to it, forming some sort of binding allegiance to it. I too, like the apostle Paul, am persuaded that the transformation is immediate, and we can begin our victorious race running because our Lord is able to keep all promises written in the Book of Life, the gospel of Jesus Christ.

Part One

~ Surely Goodness and Mercy ~

ReCoVery1

~ Assignment ~

ReCoVery

We can call on the Names of God Because our Father attests that
He is our Ever-Present Help. God is our All in All in every Challenge.
Below is a Name of God in Hebrew and the meaning.
We have access to call upon when in need.

Who is God to me Today...

Abba ~ Father

ReCoVery

Romans Chapter 1

I, Paul, a servant of Christ Jesus. God called me to be an apostle and chose me to tell the Good News. The sacred writings contain preliminary reports by the prophets on God's Son. His descent from David roots him in history; his unique identity as Son of God was shown by the Spirit when Jesus was raised from the dead, setting him apart as the Messiah, our Master. Through him we received both the generous gift of his life and the urgent task of passing it on to others who receive it by entering into obedient trust in Jesus. You are who you are through this gift and call of Jesus Christ! And I greet you now with all the generosity of God our Father and our Master Jesus, the Messiah.

—Romans 1:1 (NCV); Romans 1:2–7 (MSG)

ReCoVery

The gospel, the good news, is a victory message of glad tidings that brings joy (just one yes) to Jesus. The good news is that the power of the gospel transformed the apostle Paul's life. This change can happen to you as well, just like that. It reads in the book of Romans that the apostle Paul was originally named Saul of the city of Tarsus and he was devoted to his assignment.

You too are devoted to one thing or another, and you are also on assignment during your watch on earth. Paul's expressions in the book of Romans indicated his commitment with such a core conviction of being a servant on assignment that I was persuaded to share the multiple verses from the first fifteen chapters of Romans as a pathway through the ReCoVery process. Either you are on assignment for Jesus Christ or you are on a temporary assignment until you understand your earthly assignment. Until then, you are on assignment for the adversary.

You may choose who you want to work for or serve. Paul said that he will proclaim God's words, acts, and actions. The demonstration of your current actions, your behavior, will also exhibit what you are committed to and who you are on assignment for. Paul speaks of his authoritative position that he is authorized as an apostle to proclaim the gospel of Jesus Christ.

What is your current position in life? In Christ Jesus, as believers, we are authorized to call on the "name of Jesus." Paul stated that he writes this letter to all believers in Rome, God's friends. The Bible is written for me, you, and today. Jesus doesn't change. He is the same today, yesterday, and forever. In addition to that, every part of Scripture is God-breathed and useful one way or another—showing us truth, exposing our rebellion, correcting our mistakes, and training us to live God's way. Through the Word, we are put together and shaped for the tasks God has for us (2 Timothy 3:16–17), your assignment.

-*-Let's Reason Together -*-

We have the choice to believe in anything we want to believe in. Position yourself to turn on a light switch in a room. Wait a minute just before adjusting the switch. What do you believe is going to happen? Do you believe that the switch will make the lights come up or not? Either way, it takes faith to approach and manipulate the switch, believing in the possibility of the lights turning on versus remaining in the dark.

> "If in this life only we have hope in Christ ..."
>
> —1 Corinthians 15:19 (KJV)

ReCoVery

Paul informs us that his writings contain the preliminary reports regarding God's Son, Jesus Christ, who was raised from the dead and set apart by God as the Messiah, our Master. Through Jesus Christ, we can receive both generous gifts as the apostle Paul shared the gift of Jesus Christ's life and the gift of passing His life to others through the message of the gospel.

Immediately, once you receive these wonderful gifts from Jesus Christ, you become His friend. John 15:13–14 (AMP) reads, "no one has greater love [nor stronger commitment] than to lay down his own life for his friends. You are my friends if you keep on doing what I command you."

It is amazing how we may believe, accept, and tolerate all kinds of conditions and behaviors of ourselves, family, and friends and not question the intent. I'm attempting to persuade you to question, believe, and accept, my friend, that through the word of God, it will give you new identification, purpose, and point of reference, which points and refers others to a Savior who has designed a way to give us a rebirth experience that has no past, only a beginning of a newly transformed life.

Now, this is the icing on the cake. You are who you are through this gift. What gift? The gift of Jesus Christ's life. A renewed individual called of Jesus Christ to be on assignment in this life. Jesus Christ has designed a ReCoVery plan just for you. He was raised from the dead and born again first. Guess what? You can also become born again.

Paul stated that he so loved to worship and serve by spreading the good news of God's Son, Jesus Christ, which is the message of the gospel. Gospel means the good news. The old English version of the word "gospel" was "Godspel," meaning "the good news from God." The word was created from "good" (God is good) and "spel" (story or message). Our assignments are the two gifts mentioned previously, the gift of His life and the passing of His life through the gospel message of Christ Jesus.

~*~Let's Reason Together ~*~

The born-again experience offers a new beginning with no past, only a present and a future, a new beginning just like when you were physically born, that is, you only had a beginning. This is available to you today. You can take it from the top right now! Isn't that wonderful! We are all together with the same Abba Father, Master, Lord, Friend, and greatest Recoverer, Jesus Christ.

> "I wait in hope for your Salvation."
>
> —Genesis 49:1 (MSG)

ReCoVery

We are to worship God with our life (this life), to serve God with our life (this life), and to serve others with our life (this life) because our life is now from Jesus's life. It is of the greatest service to another to share the good news of the gospel message. You may not have yet come to a place of believing that. As a believer, I have come to this convicting faith like the apostle Paul that the gospel is the truth.

1 Peter 5:8 (KJV) reads, "Be sober, be vigilant; because your adversary the devil, as a roaring lion, walketh about, seeking whom he may devour." This Bible verse gives us a watch alert regarding the adversary for our lives because our first assignment on earth is our life. The enemy doesn't just want to hurt you; he seeks to devour you like a lion devours flesh. He thoroughly destroys his prey.

The adversary is Jesus's enemy and our enemy also. Our troublesome enemies were sin, death, and hell, but Christ conquered each of them at the cross of Calvary. These enemies were our opponents who oppose and attack our purpose to exist. These enemies deceive the world through situations, circumstances, and relationships by the way of robbery, murder, and destruction.

"And the great dragon was cast out, the serpent of old, who is called Devil and the Satan, who deceives the whole world; he was cast out into the earth, and his angels were cast out with him" (Revelation 12:9 KJV). The enemy has multiple names: the devil, the thief, and the adversary of Jesus. How interesting this very situation seems to be positioned on two opposing ends of a pendulum, life versus death. "The enemy comes to steal, to kill, and to destroy. Jesus came to give abundant life" (John 10:10 KJV), His life.

-*-Let's Reason Together -*-

If I may speculate, that gradual destruction may present slow death while being alive. The goal of the enemy is to destroy an individual before reaching their purpose at any age. However, the enemy destroys because the course of destructions robs one of life's designed purpose and function, spiraling into an unfortunate life of loss and lack.

> "Having no hope and without God in the world."
> Ephesians 2:12 (NKJV)

ReCoVery

Let's look at the surrounding circumstances of the addicted personality. This personality is compulsively obsessed and consumed with the addiction, often psychologically and physiologically unable to focus on matters of life like work, financial responsibilities, and dependability. Again, mental illnesses, sickness, diseases, and the diseased process often prevents the individual psychologically and/or physiologically unable to focus on the matters of life because they are not stable. These factors often pose a challenge to family life.

As family members persist with the burden to help, they always hope for the return of proper functional abilities good health, healthy mind, and a purpose-filled life. Unfortunately the enemy desires to devour you of your proper function to render you unusable—unusable to yourself, your family, your community, your country, the world, and the kingdom of God.

For example, one of the functions of employment, a job, or career is to give one purpose and satisfaction that an individual can provide for self and family. This position would allow one to have a dependable and reliable role as a family member and member of society. Society is a large group of people; however, the group must start with number one, two, three, and so forth. The one individual who has the problem of addiction allows the addiction to impede their glory of being a husband, father, friend, and employee in society. When magnified, this societal problem now has thousands of individuals who have problems being a husband, father, wife, mother, friend, and employee, resulting in a loss of hope, a lack of trust, and empty dreams for both the individual and the others who relied on this individual. We have a huge spiral of unfortunate situations, circumstances, and relationships.

These extenuated circumstances bring us to ReCoVery. We have pleased God by believing that He exists, and we have pleased God with our faith to make steps toward ReCoVery. Through the ReCoVery process, you decided to put your life into the way of Jesus's life. You also decided that you now want truth in your life, no more lies. Like a child when they do something right, they want to be rewarded. God is now going to reward you for your right decisions to act on your faith and act on your belief in ReCoVery.

-*-Let's Reason Together -*-

The earth and everything in it all belong to King Jesus.

> "Looking for the blessed hope and glorious appearing of great God and Savior Jesus Christ ..."
> —Titus 2:13 (NKJV)

ReCoVery

The reward is His eternal life, saved from sin, death, and hell. When we experience salvation, we are first saved from ourselves. We enjoyed our sins. The Bible reads, "the wages of sin is death; but the gift of God is eternal life through Jesus Christ our Lord" (Romans 6:23 KJV). Our new destination is with Christ, and by faith, we believe that we want to get our lives back together with Christ's help. We must remember that God first draws us to Him, and without faith, it is impossible to please God. God draws your life into His. God the Father draws people to Jesus. I believe that it's because that is the only way we will ever come.

The adversary doesn't want humanity to believe that Jesus conquered sin, death, and hell. That is why ReCoVery is not just about addiction. It is about life. ReCoVery is a constant, just like life is constant. The consequence of sin is designed to rob, kill, and destroy. Actually the enemy sets up situations, circumstances, and relationships to deceive you to kill yourself. Addiction is just one situation that spirals into multiple circumstances resulting in losses, emptiness, lack, self-hatred, heartfelt pain, depression, and thoughts of suicide. This spiraling effect occurs because the deception persuades one to think that their life is so unpleasant, they are sick and tired of being out of control, and there is no answer for help. One may tend to believe that suicide is the only way out of these unfortunate experiences. The ultimate goal of the adversary is always murder. The deception is to make the murder look like it is the result of the situations, circumstances, and relationships, but it truly is the adversary. The true word of God says, "we do not wrestle against flesh and blood, but against principalities, against powers, against the rulers of the darkness of this age, against spiritual hosts of wickedness" (Ephesian 6:12 KJV). The deception is predominantly through fear and torment of not being able to obtain the addiction of choice. This becomes one's only lifeline, the only interest twenty-four hours a day, every day.

-*-Let's Reason Together -*-

"Wanted dead or alive" is the promotion the adversary offers as a bounty for your life-your soul. He desires to render you unusable and will take you dead-dead (eternal hell) or dead-alive (internal hell)!

> "Now with hope May the God of hope fill you with all joy and peace as you trust in him, so that you may overflow by the power of the Holy Spirit."
>
> —Romans 15:13 (NIV)

ReCoVery

During multiple interviews of many individuals seeking ReCoVery, clients often make two statements when they begin the ReCoVery process. The first thing said is, "I want my life back." I wondered and sometimes asked, "Where did your life go? Who or what took your life from you?"

The second statement is, "I'm tired." Interestingly, when someone is tired, they usually stop the thing that makes them tired. If you had control, you would stop being tired and quit the unfortunate addiction, for example, drugs, cigarette smoking, pornography, pedophilia, prostitution, theft, and so forth. Addiction is a supernatural stronghold, and imprisonment that has gained control over our lives. It is beyond natural influence due to the hold. The strength of the hold is powerful. The stronghold may have originated from an interest in entertainment but eventually spiraled out of control. It is believed that you would have control over anything you choose. However, the subtle gradual growth of the appetite of desire has brought you into a place out of control.

I believe that the overall appetite of desire resulted in a taken experience. The growth of the appetite of desire has taken over your natural body for days, months, years, or decades without your acceptance awareness. It is a subtle ransom that was paid when you gave up your authority to be sober, vigilant, and watchful. That's why you want your life back. Your life had been taken out of your control. You handed over the authority of your life to the appetite of desire, ignoring the warning statement about your first assignment, your life, to be sober (unintoxicated) and vigilant (carefully observant or attentive/on the lookout for possible danger). You are the first watchman for your soul.

What happened? Initially you fought being out of control. Then there was a transition in your reasoning about the appetite of desire. You began to settle with being out of control, accepted being out of control, were consumed with being out of control, and finally conquered being overpowered by the stronghold and taken out of control.

-*-Let's Reason Together -*-
_____

The life of every person belongs to me… All souls are mind… (Ezekiel 18:4 GW/AMP)

> "Behold, the eye of the Lord is on those who fear Him,
> On those who hope in His mercy …"
>
> —Psalm 33:18 (NKJV)

ReCoVery

You are the enemy's trophy. You were taken hostage due to the levels of sin and then bound, imprisoned, and enthralled by the appetite of desire. The appetite of desire reigned over the body, controlling your life. The appetite of desire has captured your attention. The fascination of how it makes you feel has enchanted your emotions, bewitched, mesmerized, and become delightfully irresistible. This occurrence has such a subtle beginning that you don't recognize the deception. The true Word of God states that unbelief is sin. It is difficult to believe that you have allowed yourself to be taken by the addiction.

The sin of omission occurs when an individual chooses not to do what is right. Sin of commission is when an individual chooses to do what they know should not be done intentionally or unintentionally, and the presumptuous sin is intentional transgression, disobedience, and rebelliousness. The sin of iniquity becomes a daily lifestyle of evil concupiscence, forcefully propelling the appetite of desire into disaster.

God is our only answer and advocate for sin. He is our lawyer representing us; we are His client in the courtroom of heaven. He stands to our defense, interceding on the behalf of our case. The Bible reads, "I'm writing this to you so that you will not sin. Yet, if anyone does sin, we have Jesus Christ, who has God's full approval. He speaks on our behalf when we come into the presence of the Father. He is the payment for our sins, and not only for our sins, but also for the sins of the whole world" (1 John 2:1–2 GW).

~*~Let's Reason Together ~*~

Word of mouth remains to be one of the most effective forms of communication for the sharing of marketing a service. The gospel is truly a sincere service offered to humanity. When you go to church, it is often called attending a church service. The word-of-mouth exchange of communication is used predominantly by network marketing, multilevel marketing, direct selling, word-of-mouth marketing, relationship marketing, and relationship referrals. I am a network marketeer for Jesus Christ, passing on the gospel message to family, friends, and the world.[3]

> "By whom also we have access by faith into this grace wherein we stand and rejoice in hope of the glory of God. And not only so, but we glory in tribulations also: knowing that tribulation worketh patience; And patience, experience; and experience, hope: And hope maketh not ashamed; because the love of God ..."
>
> —Romans 5:1 (KJV)

ReCoVery

We can be taken by sin, all our wrongdoing/missing the mark or we can be taken by God's love and grace.

- *The Good News that we tell people may be hidden, but it is hidden only to those who are lost. The ruler of this world has blinded the minds of those who don't believe. They cannot see the light of the Good News—the message about the divine greatness of Christ. Christ is the one who is exactly like God* (2 Corinthians 4:3-4 ERV).

- *But their minds were closed. And even today, when those people read the writings of the old agreement, that same covering hides the meaning. That covering has not been removed for them. It is taken away only through Christ* (2 Corinthians 3:14 ERV).

We can relate that much is offered in this world through our desired appetite lust of flesh, lust of our eyes, and the pride of life. We desire to entertain ourselves selfishly; we want what we want through our senses visual, hearing, touch, smell, and taste. We can easily become arrogant because we believe in ourselves. The bible stated that we all have sinned. The Christian goal is maturing through daily growth and development in our belief system through the power of the gospel. It is initially necessary to consider making an effort to sin less as an ongoing part of our growth process with the help of the Holy Spirit.

-*-Let's Reason Together -*-

Have you ever watched daybreak or night fall? The transition is so subtle as its beyond your control. The twilight transition takes place right before your very eyes. It is absolutely amazing to watch! The smooth subtle deception of addiction takes place right before your very eyes. It is absolutely unfortunate to watch!

> "And endurance (fortitude) develops maturity of character (approved faith and tried integrity). And character [of this sort] produces [the habit of] joyful and confident hope of eternal salvation."
>
> Romans 5:4 -Amplified Bible-

ReCoVery

Let's Reason in Our Thoughts for a Moment...God will perfect those things that concern you.

Are there any concerns understanding the importance of being taken by loss, lack, or addictions?

- ❖   What is the situation?

- ❖   What are the circumstances?

- ❖   What is the relationship?

- ❖   ReCoVery ~ Let's get started to Rebuild.

- •   Rebuild~

- •   Rebuild together~

- •   Rebuild in truth~

ReCoVery2

~ Marvel ~

We can call on the Names of God Because our Father attests that
He is our Ever-Present Help. God is our All in All in every Challenge.
Below is a Name of God in Hebrew and the meaning.
We have access to call upon when in need.

Who is God to me Today...

Elohim ~ God

Romans Chapter 2

Those people are on a dark spiral downward. But if you think that leaves you on the high ground where you can point your finger at others, think again. Every time you criticize someone, you condemn yourself. It takes one to know one. Judgmental criticism of others is a well-known way of escaping detection in your own crimes and misdemeanors. But God isn't so easily diverted. He sees right through all such smoke screens and holds you to what you've done. You didn't think, did you, that just by pointing your finger at others you would distract God from seeing all your misdoings and from coming down on you hard?

—Romans 2:1–2 (MSG))

ReCoVery

Hero * Man: Superman, Batman, Spider-man, Iron Man, Invisible Man

Heroine * Woman: Superwoman, Catwoman, Wonder Woman

Heroin * Drugs: Morphine, Opium, Methadone, Methamphetamine, Marijuana

The superheroes are Marvel characters. There is no such thing as a superhero. It is a false deception in the mind, make-believe, a lie. Obviously, we are in need of a hero to rescue us and protect us from ourselves, self-destruction, and others. Since our original place of residence would have been paradise, we are still longing for it.

Jesus said to the thief on the cross, "today you will be with me in paradise." (Luke:23:43 NKJV) The Word of God says two things about deception: man prefers to believe the lie, and believing in the illusion of the lie, man will perish rather than receive the truth.

Two major concerns in life will sincerely hinder purpose: a lack of knowledge and disbelief. We are informed that a lack of knowledge leads to destruction. We will perish, vanish, and no longer exist because of a lack of knowledge. In the Bible, not having knowledge is synonymous with darkness. When you walk in darkness, you cannot see the path. When we are not making the best choices in our lives, we will often accompany ourselves with individuals who are not making the best choices in their lives. They can't see the right path either. We come to the realization that His life is the light that shines through the darkness that can and will show us the right path to do right.

-*-Let's Reason Together -*-

Yes, we are in need of a superhero to save the day and protect us. The only true alive marvel is Jesus Christ.

> "I wait for the Lord, my soul waits, and in His word I do hope."
>
> —Psalm 130:5 (NKJV)

ReCoVery

The Bible said that the people marveled at the miracles that Jesus did. The word "marveled" means "miracle," that is, a supernatural act of divine agency. The word "miracle" actually comes from the same Latin word as marvel. In other words, it can mean the following:

1. Be amazed at

2. Express astonishment or surprise about something

3. Something that causes feelings of wonder

See the following verses:

• "Then He arose and rebuked the winds and the sea, and there was a great calm. So the men marveled, saying, 'Who can this be, that even the winds and the sea obey Him?'" (Matthew 8:26–27 NKJV)

• "As they went out, behold, they brought to Him a man, mute and demon possessed. And when the demon was cast out, the mute spoke. And the multitudes marveled, saying, 'It was never seen like this in Israel!'" (Matthew 9:32–33 NKJV)

• "And they were all amazed at the majesty of God. But while everyone marveled at all the things which Jesus did …" (Luke 9:43 NKJV)

Jesus is not a Marvel character, but "the real marvel" that can and will protect and save the day. It's all a counterfeit compared to the real thing, Jesus Christ. Drugs make the user feel heroic, and it is often called a shortcut to paradise. Heroin is so addictive because it reaches the brain extremely fast, affecting the user psychologically and physically. The neurochemical and molecular changes in the brain take place when the drug is used, causing a rush experience to save the day. The appetite of desires becomes the rush experience to save the day, every day, every hour, every minute, and every second.

-*-Let's Reason Together -*-
_____

Jesus Christ is marvelous. He has called us out of darkness into His marvelous light.

> "Behold, the eye of the Lord is on those who fear Him,
> and those who hope in His mercy."
>
> —Psalm 33:18 (NKJV)

ReCoVery

Surges of neurochemical dopamine are produced, which is the chemical responsible for the rush of euphoria (extreme happiness: a feeling of great joy, excitement, or well-being) and pleasure experienced. The rush can be so intense that a person can't wait to achieve the rush again and again, so they repeat their use. Over time, tolerance takes place, and the dose they used in the beginning is no longer enough to reach the desired effect.[4]

The enemy is a thief and counterfeiter of all that represents Jesus Christ. For example, it is always evil versus good.

- ❖ Advocate versus Adversary
- ❖ Majestic versus Marijuana
- ❖ Angel versus Angel Dust
- ❖ The Book of Daniel versus Jack Daniels
- ❖ This is not the house that Jack built versus the house that Jesus Builds
- ❖ Christ has not given us a spirt of fear but of Sound Mind versus Mental Illnesses disorders described as phobias, obsessions, eating disorders, depression, schizophrenia, and post-traumatic stress syndrome (PTSD).[5]

There is only one Majestic One, and that is the King of Kings and Lord of Lords. "The Son is the radiance of God's glory and the exact representation of his being, sustaining all things by his powerful word. After he had provided purification for sins, he sat down at the right hand of the Majesty in heaven" (Hebrews 1:3 NIV).

There is only one place to find angels, and that is in the heavenly places on assignment by Christ protecting you and me. "Then the angel said to them, Do not be afraid, for behold, I bring you good tidings of great joy which will be to all people. For there is born to you this day in the city of David a Savior, who is Christ the Lord" (Luke 2:10–11 NKJV).

There is only one real prophesy from the book of Daniel. In Hebrew, Daniel means, "God is my judge." The American meaning of Daniel is "judgment of God." He was a Hebrew prophet whose story is told in the book of Daniel in the Old Testament. He was rewarded for the results of his actions by purposing in his heart to believe God. Daniel was rewarded when he was sentenced to the lion's den and the Lord marvelously shut the lion's mouth.

-*-Let's Reason Together -*-
_____

The enemy is a counterfeiter who "deceives the whole world" (Revelation 12:9 NKJV).

> "Therefore my heart is glad, and my glory rejoices; My flesh also will rest in hope."
> —Psalm 16:9 (NKJV)

ReCoVery

The poor physically and the poor at heart are the same in Christ's sight. More importantly, the poor that Christ references is the one who is poor due to an overall loss of life without Jesus Christ. The only paradise that man-to-man can ever offer is material wealth. But God offers what all people are looking for; rather they are wealthy or poor, both monetarily and poor at heart. And that is to live forever in paradise. The fountain of youth is forever sought after in the hope to acquire the formula for long life. Paradise is sought after through various ways, for example, one's private home, a trip to the most expensive day spa or exotic beach resort, all kinds of addictions, or a belief in superheroes to save the day.

Have you ever heard written in a movie script the following: a commercialized superhero saying to the victim who was rescued after conquering the villain, "I love you"? In man's eye, paradise is equated with riches, fame, prestige, and power. But Christ Jesus equates paradise with His love, protection, deliverance, rescue for humanity from humanity, and eternal life in paradise with Him. Of the two criminals who hang on the cross with Jesus, one of them asked, "Jesus remember me when you come into your kingdom. Jesus reply, truly I tell you today you will be with me in paradise" (Luke 23:43 NKJV).

-*-Let's Reason Together -*-

Any good news is always good. The good news of God is always good.

> "For in You, O Lord, I hope; You will hear, O Lord my God."
>
> —Psalm 38:15 (NKJV)

ReCoVery

The repenting thief, one of the criminals hanging on the cross next to Jesus, asked, "I beg of you, Jesus, show me grace and take me with you into your everlasting kingdom!" Jesus responded, "I promise you this very day you will enter paradise with me" (Luke 23:41–43 TPT). This simple exchange instructs mankind how to get to paradise by simply asking Jesus.

The kingdom of God is paradise. "Thy kingdom come, thy will be done, on earth as it is in Heaven" (Matthew 6:10 KJV). Heaven is the only paradise that will ever be found. It may be found through Christ Jesus. Jesus prepares a place for us in His Father's home. He informs us that His Father has many mansions waiting for our arrival. Jesus tells us in the Word, "I'm on my way to get a room ready for you. And if I'm on my way to get your room ready, I'll be back and get you so you can live where I live" (John 14:2–4 MSG). Jesus asks us, "Do we know the way to paradise?"

Let's review how the Bible describes paradise.

> There will be brightness forever illuminated by the presences of Christ Jesus. There will not be night. God will wipe away every tear from their eyes; there shall be no more death, nor sorrow, nor crying. There shall be no more pain, for the former things have passed away … The construction of its wall was of jasper; and the city was pure gold, like clear glass. The foundations of the wall of the city were adorned with all kinds of precious stones: the first foundation was jasper, the second sapphire, the third chalcedony, the fourth emerald, the fifth sardonyx, the sixth sardius, the seventh chrysolite, the eighth beryl, the ninth topaz, the tenth chrysoprase, the eleventh jacinth, and the twelfth amethyst. The twelve gates were twelve pearls: each individual gate was of one pearl. And the street of the city was pure gold, like transparent glass. But I saw no temple in it, for the Lord God Almighty and the Lamb are its temple. The city had no need of the sun or of the moon to shine in it, for the glory of God illuminated it. The Lamb is its light. And the nations of those who are saved shall walk in its light, and the kings of the earth bring their glory and honor into it. Its gates shall not be shut at all by day, there shall be no night there. And they shall bring the glory and the honor of the nations into it. But there shall by no means enter it anything that defiles, or causes an abomination or a lie, but only those who are written in the Lamb's Book of Life (Revelation 21:4, 18–27 NKJV).

-*-Let's Reason Together -*-

Since God breathes into man the breath of life, it would make sense that God would also monitor, maintain, and manage that precious breath of life that He has given to each of us.

> "Why are you cast down, O my soul? And why are you disquieted within me?
> Hope in God, for I shall yet praise Him For the help of His countenance."
>
> —Psalm 42:5 (NKJV)

ReCoVery

Let's Reason in Our Thoughts for a Moment... God will perfect those things that concern you.

Are there any concerns understanding the importance to be rescued and protected from yourself and others?

- ❖ What is the situation?

- ❖ What are the circumstances?

- ❖ What is the relationship?

- ❖ ReCoVery ~ Let's get started to Rebuild.

- • Rebuild~

- • Rebuild together~

- • Rebuild in truth~

ReCoVery3

~ Charged ~

ReCoVery

We can call on the Names of God Because our Father attests that
He is our Ever-Present Help. God is our All in All in every Challenge.
Below is a Name of God in Hebrew and the meaning.
We have access to call upon when in need.

Who is God to me Today...

Yahweh ~ Lord, Jehovah

Romans Chapter 3

God sacrificed Jesus on the altar of the world to clear that world of sin. Having faith in him sets us in the clear. God decided on this course of action in full view of the public—to set the world in the clear with himself through the sacrifice of Jesus, finally taking care of the sins he had so patiently endured. This is not only clear, but it's now—this is current history! God sets things right. He also makes it possible for us to live in his rightness.

—Romans 3:25–26 (MSG)

ReCoVery

I'm not ashamed of the gospel because it is the good news of Jesus Christ. It is God's power to save everyone who believes, Jews first and everybody as well. God's approval is revealed in this good news. This approval begins and ends with faith, as Scripture says, "The person who has God's approval will live by faith" (Romans 1:17 GW).

All of humanity and the fullness of the earth were created by the one God. The Bible states that humanity is a little lower than angels and we are given glory and honor crowned by Christ. The adversary is a fallen angel attacking our purpose. Since we are a little lower than fallen angels, how does this factor position humanity for defending ourselves against demonic attacks? To make the earth meaningful and purposeful for humanity; God has made all things work together for good for those who love God and for those who are called according to His purpose.

Why would it be significant that all things work together? Why didn't God just make some things work together? Because Christ is knowledgeable of the fiery darts of the adversary. Christ knows that the adversary has only one plan for humanity, murder through robbery and destruction, utilizing deceptive situations, circumstances, and relationships. When we are in a place of calling according to His purpose, our footsteps are ordered, and what the adversary meant for evil, the Lord turns it around for our good. As we grow in our Christian life, we learn that under the call, our God accordingly supplies us with weapons to assist in our protection against the adversary that helps us allay his attacks.

For example, these weapons are called the armor of God. Armor is weaponry of war. It is our full Christian military combat attire. This armor strengthens us with Christ strength while giving us the stability to stand face-to-face against the adversary deception, which the Bible calls the wiles of the devil. This armor is not invisible, but it is an armor of integrity of moral and ethical soundness: live in the truth, do right to yourself and others, have peace about yourself that comes from God, have faith in Jesus for your ReCoVery success, allow yourself to believe in the salvation of Jesus Christ, study the Bible to acquire understanding, and pray to Christ with your whole heart for everything. The enemy doesn't like a decision based on integrity; his preference is deceitfulness, distortion of the truth, dishonesty, and corruption.

-*-Let's Reason Together -*-

God will give you a good and honest life.

> "All people will hope in him."
>
> —Matthew 12:21 (ERV)

ReCoVery

We must learn to love God by falling in love with Him. We must believe that we are called for His purpose. Christ will help us when we are weak. Christ also tells us that Christians can do exceedingly great things because Christ makes us greater when He lives on the inside of us. The adversary doesn't want us to believe that we were designed to have a great life assisted and protected by God. We are more than conquerors. *We are of the utmost significance in that we are the only creature made in our Father's likeness. We have the mind of Christ with earthly authority to rule, serve, and conquer our enemies of anxiety, fear, and torment.* Any form of addiction has an element of torment derived from the fear of being out of control and the overwhelming thought of not being able to obtain the thing that drives that behavior. The torment leads to feelings of anguish and hurt, leading to psychological and physiological pain. Let the ReCoVery process of Jesus Christ work its purpose.

~*~Let's Reason Together ~*~

Our God is God, supernatural Omni-God, God in nature, and God in character.

- Omnipresent: All-Present
- Omniscient: All-Knowing
- Omnipotent: All-Powerful
- Omnificent: All Creative Power
- Omnibenevolent: All-Loving

> "The Lord is my portion, says my soul, Therefore I hope in Him!"
> —Lamentations 3:24 (NKJV)

ReCoVery

The subtitle specifically states that we have been charged of sin. The entire human race is united under this umbrella. We are all united in this life together by this one charge called sin. From these verses found in chapter three, we can turn each of these statements into a question pertaining to life from Romans 3:10–18 (AMP).

- ❖ There is none righteous, no, not one
  - ➤ Is there one who does right in this life?
- ❖ There is none who understands
  - ➤ Is there one who understands this life?
- ❖ There is none who seeks after God
  - ➤ Is there one who seeks after God in this life?
- ❖ They have all turned aside
  - ➤ Is there one who has not turned aside from God in this life?
- ❖ They have together become unprofitable
  - ➤ Have we together become unprofitable in this life?
- ❖ There is none who does good, no, not one
  - ➤ Is there one who does good in this life? Is there One? Is it you?
- ❖ Their throat is an open tomb
  - ➤ Are you ready to swallow up the innocent, captives, blind, poor, brokenhearted prisoners, those who are bound and oppressed in this life?
- ❖ With their tongues, they have practiced deceit
  - ➤ Have you practiced deceit in this life?
- ❖ The poison of asps is under their lips
  - ➤ With poisonous words, do we slander one another in this life?
- ❖ Whose mouth is full of cursing and bitterness
  - ➤ Is your mouth full of cursing and bitterness in this life?
- ❖ Their feet are swift to shed blood
  - ➤ Are your feet swift to shed the blood of others in life?
- ❖ Destruction and misery are in their ways
  - ➤ Do you behave in a destructive, miserable manner in this life?
- ❖ The way of peace they have not known
  - ➤ Do you know peace in this life?
- ❖ There is no fear of God before their eyes
  - ➤ Do you have the fear of God in your eyes in this life?

-*-Let's Reason Together -*-
_____

Do you have a healthy fear of God in this life?

> "But let us who are of the day be sober, putting on the breastplate of faith and love, and as a helmet the hope of salvation."
>
> —1 Thessalonians 5:8 (NKJV)

ReCoVery

Let's Reason in Our Thoughts for a Moment... God will perfect those things that concern you.

Are there any concerns understanding the significance of Christianity that we are the only creatures made in our Father's likeness; having the mind of Christ with earthly authority to live, rule, serve; and enabling us to conqueror our enemies of anxiety, fear, and torment.

❖ What is the situation?

❖ What are the circumstances?

❖ What is the relationship?

❖ ReCoVery - Let's get started to Rebuild.

• Rebuild-

• Rebuild together-

• Rebuild in truth-

ReCoVery4

~Betrayal~

ReCoVery

We can call on the Names of God Because our Father attests that
He is our Ever-Present Help. God is our All in All in every Challenge.
Below is a Name of God in Hebrew and the meaning.
We have access to call upon when in need.

Who is God to me Today...

Adonai ~ Lord, Master

Romans Chapter 4

What we read in Scripture is, "Abraham entered into what God was doing for him, and that was the turning point. He trusted God to set him right instead of trying to be right on his own." If you're a hard worker and do a good job, you deserve your pay; we don't call your wages a gift. But if you see that the job is too big for you, that it's something only God can do, and you trust him to do it—you could never do it for yourself no matter how hard and long you worked—well, that trusting-him-to-do-it is what gets you set right with God, by God. Sheer gift.

—Romans 4:3–5 (MSG)

ReCoVery

Paul said Abraham "entered into what God was doing for him resulting in a turning point" (Romans 4:4 MSG). The turning point of your actions for your life is to enter into what God has for you by trusting God with your life choices. The next question is, "What has Christ done for you?" The Word of God stated that while Jesus was on the cross, He knowingly and officially announced to the public that through Him all things were now accomplished. Jesus said, "it is finished" (John 19:28–30 AMP).

What was accomplished, and what was finished? Everything. He has set you free from everything that you have been persuaded to believe that is hurtful to your life. With Christ being trustworthy, we can rest with assurance He is able to resolve every problem in our lives because it was all dealt with at Calvary. He can heal the brokenhearted, deliver captives, and complete ReCoVery of sight of both the blind physiological and poorly blind at heart. Positive turning points in life have the hope to set things right in your life. We may opt to think that setting things right after much loss, confusion, and heartbreak is too big to handle. We serve a God that handles all things for us. For example, the rejection and loss of a spouse through divorce affects both individuals brokenheartedly.

Malachi 2:16 (NRSV) reads, "for I hate divorce, says the Lord, the God of Israel, and covering one's garment with violence says the Lord of hosts. So take heed to yourselves and do not be faithless." The turning point of a divorce doesn't begin in the courtroom. Divorce begins with individuals acting out what is in their hearts. What makes divorce cruel and violent? Deception. The thought process is just like the betrayal between Jesus and Judas Iscariot, the apostle who betrayed Jesus. Judas Iscariot thought his decision was the right thing to do for him and him alone. Did Judas Iscariot and the divorcing couple guard their hearts as instructed in the book of Malachi?

-*-Let's Reason Together -*-

Every lie begins with you! You must convince yourself first that the lie will carry out its purpose.

> "Through whom also we have access by faith into this grace in which we stand and rejoice in hope of the glory of God. Jesus Christ …"
>
> —Romans 5:2 (NKJV)

ReCoVery

He did not consider the others whom he lived, ate, and fellowshipped with. The twelve apostles grew to love one another and cared for one another and Jesus. Judas Iscariot's identification of Jesus with a kiss was a breach of friendship. Did Judas Iscariot understand the breach of his own identity at that very moment? Judas Iscariot had already lost connection and commitment and had divorced Jesus in his heart before the day he identified Him.

Loss can often change identification and directions. Jesus had identified who Judas Iscariot was in His life and amongst the others. It is written in the Bible that if you think of a thing in your thought process, you have already committed it. Judas Iscariot's progressive sin nature had to mobilize itself to the last level of sin to carry out such a cruel, violent, and hurtful deed of homicide against Jesus.

It is written that Satan entered Judas Iscariot just before he went to agree that he would be the one who identified Christ for a monetary payment. Judas Iscariot changed his own identity from an apostle, a man of God, to an apostate not believing in God, from a man of faith to one that rejected repentance. His character was that of a betrayal and a counterfeiter of deception. He entertained and later endorsed thoughts of homicidal and suicidal ideations. He hung himself due to deep regret for the surrounding circumstances of his act of betrayal. Finally, Judas Iscariot violently ended his own life by hanging himself. His entire body burst into flames, and all bodily intestines pooled outside of him onto the ground. That was the price he paid for thirty pieces of silver. What a cruel and violent retribution. This is a prime example that God will improve or remove them.

The end result of his wages, payment, or payoff for identifying Jesus was death due to lack of repentance and brokenheartedness. I believe that both Jesus and Judas were brokenhearted over the sad, unfortunate circumstances of betrayer. Jesus also said that He is married to the backslider, a person who relapses in their old, negative ways. Jesus felt sorrow of a father and friend, watching what was once a loving relationship go down the wrong road.

-*-Let's Reason Together -*-
_____

With Christ, all things are possible!

> "My soul gave up all hope, but then I remembered the Lord. I prayed to you, and you heard my prayers in your holy Temple."
>
> —Jonah 2:7 (ERV)

44

ReCoVery

The married couple's identification has changed from married to divorce, and possibly name identification has changed for the wife if she returns to her maiden name. The Word of God mentions that there would be a rebellious falling away from the true word of God. Humanity will further reject the truth of the gospel of Jesus Christ. We are living in America, the land of the free and free religion versus other lands, where worshipping our Christian faith could cost an individual their life. It's ironic as I investigated the state of apostasy. I read that in the Islamic religion, the penalty for committing apostasy is a penalty of death in addition to other penalties similar to divorce proceedings in America, enforced annulment of a person's marriage, seizure of one's children, and property with automatic assignment of guardianship and heirs.[6]

Jesus is saying to the couples, "You are heading down the wrong road due to unforgiveness." There will be an annulment of the marriage and a seizure of properties until all items are settled, and the court will assign parental guardianship of the children-heirs. The challenge is to arrest the pain, hurt, and not fall into the deception- which is extremely hard. However, what is addressed here is that faith in Jesus Christ can change the outcome of the situation more than any other factor. Christ stated that all one needs is faith as small as a mustard seed. Therefore, you may have unbelief about how it looks and feels at a given moment, but you only need a small amount of faith to accomplish your desire to believe in not going down a road of regrets. Again, like Judas Iscariot only thinking about himself, the divorcing individuals are only thinking about the hurt they are feeling, which is understandable. Jesus desires for husbands and wives to raise their children together in a Christian home for the length of life.

Not only did Judas Iscariot betray Jesus, but it reads in Matthew 26 that each of the remaining disciples forsook Christ as well at His arrest prior to going to the cross of Calvary. But Jesus recovered as He proceeded to the cross of Calvary with purpose and commitment for the souls of mankind, and you too can recover. The fight is always for the souls of mankind.

-*-Let's Reason Together -*-

Jesus will always send you help!

> "Therefore my heart rejoiced, and my tongue was glad;
> Moreover my flesh also will rest in hope."
>
> —Acts 2:26 (NKJV)

ReCoVery

Let's Reason in Our Thoughts for a Moment...God will perfect those things that concern you.

Are there any concerns understanding betrayal and broken heartiness?

- ❖ What is the situation?

- ❖ What are the circumstances?

- ❖ What is the relationship?

- ❖ ReCoVery ~ Let's get started to Rebuild.

- • Rebuild~

- • Rebuild together~

- • Rebuild in truth ~

ReCoVery

The Ten Commandments

Old and New Testaments Findings of the Ten Commandments
The first five commandments pertain to man's relationship with God;
the other five pertain to man's relationship with one another.

1. "You shall have no other gods before Me." (Exodus 20:3 NKJV)
   - "You shall worship the Lord your God and Him alone shall you serve." (Matthew 4:10; 1 Corinthians 8:4–6 NKJV)
2. "You shall not make for yourself a carved image—any likeness of anything that is in heaven above, or that is in the earth beneath, or that is in the water under the earth: you shall not bow down to them nor serve them …" (Exodus 20:4–5 NKJV)
   - "Little children, keep yourselves from idols." (1 John 5:21; Acts 17:29 NKJV)
3. "You shall not take the name of the Lord your God in vain, for the Lord will not hold him guiltless who takes His name in vain." (Exodus 20:7 NKJV)
   - "Our Father Who is in heaven, hallowed be Your name …" (Matthew 6:9; 1 Timothy 6:1 NKJV)
4. "Remember the Sabbath day, to keep it holy …" (Exodus 20:8–11 NKJV).
   - "The Sabbath was made for man, and not man for the Sabbath; Therefore, the Son of man is Lord even of the Sabbath." (Mark 2:27–28; Hebrews 4:4, 10; Acts 17:2 NKJV)
5. "Honor your father and your mother …" (Exodus 20:12 NKJV)
   - "Honor your father and your mother." (Matthew 19:19; Ephesians 6:1 NKJV)
6. "You shall not murder." (Exodus 20:13 NKJV)
   - "You shall not murder." (Matthew 19:18; Romans 13:9; Revelation 21:8 NKJV)
7. "You shall not commit adultery." (Exodus 20:14 NKJV)
   - "You shall not commit adultery." (Matthew 19:18; Romans 13:9; Revelation 21:8 NKJV)
8. "You shall not steal." (Exodus 20:15 NKJV)
   - "You shall not steal." (Matthew 19:18; Romans 13:9 NKJV)
9. "You shall not bear false witness against your neighbor." (Exodus 20:16 NKJV)
   - "You shall not bear false witness." (Matthew 19:18; Romans 13:9; Revelation 21:8 NKJV)
10. "You shall not covet your neighbor's house … your neighbor's wife … nor anything that is your neighbor's." (Exodus 20:17; Romans 13:9 NKJV)
    - "You shall not covet." (Romans 13:9; Romans 7:7 NKJV)

Part Two

~ Shall Follow Me~

ReCoVery5

~ Responsibilities ~

We can call on the Names of God Because our Father attests that
He is our Ever-Present Help. God is our All in All in every Challenge.
Below is a Name of God in Hebrew and the meaning.
We have access to call upon when in need.

Who is God to me Today…

El Shaddai ~ Lord God Almighty

Romans Chapter 5

Yet the rescuing gift is not exactly parallel to the death-dealing sin. If one man's sin put crowds of people at the dead-end abyss of separation from God, just think what God's gift poured through one man, Jesus Christ, will do! There's no comparison between that death-dealing sin and this generous, life-giving gift. The verdict on that one sin was the death sentence; the verdict on the many sins that followed was this wonderful life sentence. If death got the upper hand through one man's wrongdoing, can you imagine the breathtaking recovery life makes, sovereign life, in those who grasp with both hands this wildly extravagant life-gift, this grand setting-everything-right, that the one man Jesus Christ provides?!

—Romans 5:15–17 (MSG)

ReCoVery

Christ's desire is to always do for us, set us right with Him, and make us fit for Him. All parents desire and delight in doing for their children. Parents desire to have a right relationship with their children and hope to assist in setting their children ready for life. What better way to be set right and fit for God as we throw open our doors to receive Him as our personal Lord and Savior. His ReCoVery plan has already been set for us. At the same time you receive Christ, Christ receives you unto reconciliation to Him.

Now that is a ReCoVery plan! His plan is set immediately to assist us in the rebuilding phases of life: "Re" (rebuilding of losses), "Co" (together with Him because He is now personally involved in your life choices), and "Very" ("very" the adjective meaning the exact, precise, perfect, and truth; "very" the adverb meaning in a high degree, exceedingly, extremely, and exceptionally). In His exceeding truth, which has set you free from emptiness, lack, and disappointments. You are now equipped with the glory of the Trinity—the Father, the Son, and the Holy Spirit—all living on the inside of you with the grace of God poured into you for a victorious life.

What is for God's glory is for our glory also. (Glory translates to dignity, honor, praise, worship, and the Anointing, the Holy Spirit.) We were created for God's glory. So our glory is what God created us for, to be, and to do by His design. We were created to be man and woman for God's glory and our glory. We are to be a man and women with dignity about ourselves to praise and worship God with our lives honorable. We were created to be husbands and wives to multiply for God's glory and our glory.

-*-Let's Reason Together -*-

You are set free and equipped with the impartation endowed of all that you need in this life, the kingdom of God, the Trinity: the Father, the Son, and the Holy Spirit. The greater one lives on the inside of us, which is greater than anything in this world.

- "For indeed, the kingdom of God is within you ..." (Luke 17:20–21 NKJV)
- God has said: "I will live in them ..." (2 Corinthians 6:16 NLV)
- "The secret is this: Christ in you." (Colossians 1:27 NLV)
- "The Holy Spirit and He lives in you ..." (1 John 2:27 NLV)
- "You are of God and you belong to Him and have overcome them, because the one who is in you is greater than the one who is in the world ..." (1 John 4:4 AMP)

> "We thank God for the hope that is being kept for you in heaven. You first heard about this hope through the Good News which is the Word of Truth."
> —Colossians 1:5 (NLV)

ReCoVery

We are to be husbands and wives with dignity to praise and worship God with our marriages honorable. We were created to rest and sleep (on the seventh day, Sabbath) for God's glory and our glory. We need rest and sleep to function properly. We were created to be creative, creating with our minds and hands for ourselves and others for God's glory and our glory. We were created to serve and worship God for His glory and our glory, bringing us into His presence. We were created to glorify God in our work and ministries. We are to long enjoy the work of hands to glorify Jesus Christ with our lives in the presence of His Shekinah glory, Hebrew for "God presence on earth."

How dramatic the announcement in the book of Genesis, "In the beginning God …" From that statement, one can envision the beginning of a story. This was the introductory statement to the entire Bible. Then the very next thing God does is create all that humanity has ever heard about all the days of their lives. God created the heavens and the earth in all His glory, honor, and majesty. Who does that? Who can do such a thing? How did He create the heavens and the earth? God not only gives an explanation how. He demonstrates how. He spoke it into existence. God said, and it was.

That is what humanity does during their every awakening hour of the day, speak. We talk all day long. Our God spoke everything into existence. What a grave demonstration of His glory. It reads in the Bible that God will not share His glory, not our crowned glory, but His majestic glory of being God, with no one.

Can we look at Jonah's dilemma for a moment? It is the story of Jonah inside the big fish due to rebelliousness of refusing his assignment. Jonah immediately confessed that all the travelers' troubles that they were experiencing from the storm would immediately cease once he left the ship. And the only place to exit was into the deep. Jonah ran from his God's ordained assignment. God didn't stop him at the initial point of flight. He allowed the plot to develop because God's glory is glorified from fully detailed testimonies, a story with all the five elements of a story: character, plot, setting, conflict, and theme.

-*-Let's Reason Together -*-

Jesus Christ's love is better than life.

"There is one body and one Spirit, just as you were called in one hope of your calling …"
—Ephesians 4:4 (NKJV)

ReCoVery

All of humanity enjoys a good story, and obviously so does God. We learn to acquire an appreciation for reading and storytelling at an early age, starting with nightly stories and going to the library storytelling from toddlers throughout childhood. We learn to engage in story time as children all through our lives, as reading is fundamental. The elderly love the limelight of telling young people their stories.

Interestingly, most animals don't have the ability to converse. They can only mimic human sounds probably due to a lack of intellect. There are known animals that mimic human sounds: birds, elephants, orangutans, dolphins, and whales.[7]

The Bible records of two additional animals that both held cognizant conversations with humans. The serpent talked to Eve in the garden in the book of Genesis, and Balaam's donkey spoke to him in the book of Numbers. Jonah's experience inside the big fish was a supernatural encounter that God allowed.

God will always get the glory for one's life testimony. Who could do it like God? God purposed the big fish to swallow and regurgitate Jonah at a given time. God glorified Himself by allowing the experience, and then He honored Himself by providing the rescue. God chose one of the listed animals that have some intelligence. The big fish could have been a dolphin or whale. They have the intelligence to mimic human sounds. Eve (Genesis 3) and Balaam (Numbers 22) both experienced supernatural conversations with animals, the serpent and donkey. Why? So God may show His amazing glory and honor, filling the story with supernatural facts that present His glorious details. I love the Lord! God told Jonah that He relented on His threat of destruction from the people of Nineveh because He lovingly pities humanity that does not know the difference between wrong or right and is no better than mere animals. This account is found in the book of Jonah.

-*-Let's Reason Together -*-

The truth reads that the word of God is settled in heaven and earth and has been established throughout every generation.

> "To them God willed to make known what are the riches of the glory of this mystery among the Gentiles: which is Christ in you, the hope of glory."
> —Colossians 1:27 (NKJV)

ReCoVery

Let's Reason in Our Thoughts for a Moment... God will perfect those things that concern you.

Are there any concerns understanding importance of not running away from your responsibilities?

- ❖ What is the situation?

- ❖ What are the circumstances?

- ❖ What is the relationship?

- ❖ ReCoVery ~ Let's get started to Rebuild.

  - • Rebuild~

  - • Rebuild together~

  - • Rebuild in truth~

ReCoVery6

~ *Escape* ~

ReCoVery

We can call on the Names of God Because our Father attests that
He is our Ever-Present Help. God is our All in All in every Challenge.
Below is a Name of God in Hebrew and the meaning.
We have access to call upon when in need.

Who is God to me Today...

El Elyon ~ The Most High God

ReCoVery

Romans Chapter 6

So what do we do? Keep on sinning so God can keep on forgiving? I should hope not! If we've left the country where sin is sovereign, how can we still live in our old house there? Or didn't you realize we packed up and left there for good? That is what happened in baptism. When we went under the water, we left the old country of sin behind; when we came up out of the water, we entered into the new country of grace—a new life in a new land! That's what baptism into the life of Jesus means. When we are lowered into the water, it is like the burial of Jesus; when we are raised up out of the water, it is like the resurrection of Jesus. Each of us is raised into a light-filled world by our Father so that we can see where we're going in our new grace-sovereign country. Could it be any clearer? Our old way of life was nailed to the cross with Christ, a decisive end to that sin-miserable life—no longer at sin's every beck and call! What we believe is this: If we get included in Christ's sin-conquering death, we also get included in his life-saving resurrection. We know that when Jesus was raised from the dead it was a signal of the end of death-as-the-end. Never again will death have the last word. When Jesus died, he took sin down with him, but alive he brings God down to us. From now on, think of it this way: Sin speaks a dead language that means nothing to you; God speaks your mother tongue, and you hang on every word. You are dead to sin and alive to God. That's what Jesus did. That means you must not give sin a vote in the way you conduct your lives. Don't give it the time of day. Don't even run little errands that are connected with that old way of life. Throw yourselves wholeheartedly and full-time—remember, you've been raised from the dead!—into God's way of doing things. Sin can't tell you how to live. After all, you're not living under that old tyranny any longer. You're living in the freedom of God.

—Romans 6:1–14 (MSG)

ReCoVery

Acts 17:28 reads, "in Him we live, move, and have our being." In this verse, "being" is associated with living and movement. When we accept Jesus Christ as our Savior, old things are taken away because we have become new, hence born-again. Our being is transformed anew. We can take it from the top, no past, only a future for our new life. The symbolism of the resurrection is the water baptism. That is when we have submerged our old ways under the water and come upward with a new life, a new movement, and a new being. The resurrection is significant of the transition from a life of doing what you want to do, to grow in a loving response to do for Christ. The words "resurrection" and "resuscitate" both have similar meaning, to revive a recovering of life. Christ has resuscitated us back to life through His resurrection power. He has revived us through reconciliation, giving us restitution of all that the enemy has stolen. He has recompensed your losses back to the rightful owner, you! He has satisfied your losses by de-thralling the enemy's hold and removing all negative invested interest you may have had in the past.

It is the exact same power that resurrected Christ on the third day after the cross experience on the hill of Calvary in Jerusalem. The act of resurrection and resuscitation represents a forward movement. It would be unusual to want to go backward into a lifeless state. Is it impossible to stay focused on driving a car forward when your head is turned looking backward?

I believe that God says to your new life, "I rescued you, and I saved you from tribulations and distress. Now I desire to do a new thing in your life, and I deeply want you to take Me at My word, literally. I just want you to look ahead from now on and believe in Me for daily guidance. Don't look back at your past because you are in Me. I am in you. I am the resurrection and the life you now have."

We are to trust God for our new direction with new movement to get there. Our King will always provide a way of escape due to His faithfulness. There is no need to look back but rejoice for the chance to engage in the ReCoVery of all losses.

There is an intriguing Bible story about a man name Lot. Lot and his family had to leave the town they were living in immediately to escape mass destruction because the people of that city cried out to the Lord for His assistance.

-*-Let's Reason Together -*-

The baptism into the life of Jesus is when we are lowered into the water. It is like or symbolic of the burial of Jesus. When we are raised up out of the water, it is like or symbolic of the resurrection of Jesus.

> "A war horse is a false hope for salvation; and by its great might it cannot rescue you."
> —Psalm 33:17 (ESV)

ReCoVery

People usually cry out to God when something concerns them that is not right in their lives, just like we do. The town was involved in sexual promiscuity and perversion. God sent His angels to verify that the outcry held truth and validity against the people in the town before He made His final decision. But before the destruction of the town, the angel actually took Lot, Lot's wife, and Lot's daughters by the hand and literally led them to a place of safety. "The LORD being merciful to him, and they brought him out and set him outside the city" (Genesis 19:16).

God expressed exceedingly great mercy to send the angels to warn them. But was that not enough to be taken to a place of protection and safety by an angel? In addition, the angels gave the Lot family further warning instructions. They were not to look backward toward the town, as they were moving forward away from danger.

Lot and his two daughters escaped the situation. But unfortunately Lot's wife probably did not feel secure about the decision and was saddened to leave her home. She turned to look back, and unfortunately due to disobedience, God turned her into a pillar of salt. I believe she lost her being due to desiring the things of the past that were most familiar. She lacked the faith to trust God for guidance and disbelieved that the direction was the correct way designed by God.

Why a pillar of salt? I'm not sure. Possibly the power and grace of being given a second chance is the resolution of a transformation into salt versus the transformation of a better covenant with God. To take for granted that Christ just owes you a better life shares an air of arrogance. There is nothing in this life that is owed to anyone. Christ gave His life so we may have a better life on earth and in heaven with Him.

Faith is sometimes understandably scary because it is the unknown. Humanity does not have much appreciation for the unknown. It is something hoped for without any evidence that it is the right move. Christ, our heavenly Father, and earthly parents deeply desire that their children would just take their word about some matters of life to avoid and escape dire consequences, but that is not always the case. Despite living with parents a great deal of their lives, children and young adults often refuse to obey parental instructions and good advice. That is why it is necessary to exchange our old desires for God's new desires and to do life God's way. He is the way, the way to truth, and the way to a better life.

-*-Let's Reason Together -*-
_____

Now that you have accepted Christ as your personal Savior with the benefit of grace, can you live any way you want or do anything that comes to your mind?

> "Without ceasing, remembering your effectual faith, and diligent love, and the patience of your hope in our Lord Jesus Christ, in the sight of God, even our Father, Knowing, beloved brethren, that ye are elect of God."
>
> —1 Thessalonians 1:3–4 (GNV)

ReCoVery

<u>Let's Reason in Our Thoughts for a Moment</u>... God will perfect those things that concern you.

Are there any concerns understanding the importance of how to better avoid and escape dire consequences in your life?

- ❖ What is the situation?

- ❖ What are the circumstances?

- ❖ What is the relationship?

- ❖ ReCoVery - Let's get started to Rebuild.

- • Rebuild-

- • Rebuild together-

- • Rebuild in truth-

ReCoVery7

~ Pleasure ~

We can call on the Names of God Because our Father attests that
He is our Ever-Present Help. God is our All in All in every Challenge.
Below is a Name of God in Hebrew and the meaning.
We have access to call upon when in need.

Who is God to me Today...

El Olam ~ The Everlasting God

ReCoVery

Romans Chapter 7

I can anticipate the response that is coming: "I know that all God's commands are spiritual, but I'm not. Isn't this also your experience?" Yes. I'm full of myself—after all, I've spent a long time in sin's prison. What I don't understand about myself is that I decide one way, but then I act another, doing things I absolutely despise. So if I can't be trusted to figure out what is best for myself and then do it, it becomes obvious that God's command is necessary. But I need something more! For if I know the law but still can't keep it, and if the power of sin within me keeps sabotaging my best intentions, I obviously need help! I realize that I don't have what it takes. I can will it, but I can't do it. I decide to do good, but I don't really do it; I decide not to do bad, but then I do it anyway. My decisions, such as they are, don't result in actions. Something has gone wrong deep within me and gets the better of me every time. It happens so regularly that it's predictable. The moment I decide to do good, sin is there to trip me up. I truly delight in God's commands, but it's pretty obvious that not all of me joins in that delight. Parts of me covertly rebel, and just when I least expect it, they take charge. I've tried everything and nothing helps. I'm at the end of my rope. Is there no one who can do anything for me? Isn't that the real question? The answer, thank God, is that Jesus Christ can and does. He acted to set things right in this life of contradictions where I want to serve God with all my heart and mind but am pulled by the influence of sin to do something totally different.

—Romans 7:14–25 (MSG)

ReCoVery

When I first came into my born-again life, I read Romans 7 and thought retrospectively about my life that it was unbelievably true about me. I enjoyed and delightfully indulged in the sin of my choice to such a degree that nothing else mattered, nothing was more important, and nothing took the place of that immediate pleasure. I was therefore willing to risk anything and everything, even to the point of destroying myself and relationships, loving, respectful relationships of mother, father, sister, brother, friend, community, and others. I assessed my deep-rooted selfish rebelliousness and decided to define sin for myself as immediate gratifications at the expense of self and others. For Christ came for this very reason to help me in my sin-sick soul. Our souls are sick, for the cure that Jesus gives us by recovering us from ourselves to a place of green pasture that He makes us lie down in. He must make us lie down because we prefer to remain where we are. He does this by helping us give up selfish gratification. We have all fallen short of God's glory, not His expectation of us, but we exhibit a lack of appreciation of His grace.

The story of Samson found in Judges 16 is about the relationship of how Samson was intrigued by a woman named Delilah. This story has the trace elements of why we insist on doing things that will lead us down the wrong road despite visible and tangible warnings. When confronted with the challenges of why we do it anyway, could this be an inclination that something is out of control? Samson is in love with Delilah, but is Delilah in love with Samson? Some relationships are costly and deadly. I'm of the belief that Sampson wanted to serve God with all his heart and mind, but he was pulled by the influence of Delilah. I believe that everyone has a margin of influence on others by design. This influence can and will often border on the cusp of good and evil.

~*~Let's Reason Together ~*~
_____

And nothing took the place of my immediate pleasure!

> "So prepare your minds for service. With complete self-control put all your hope in the grace that will be yours when Jesus Chris come."
>
> —1 Peter 1:13 (ERV)

ReCoVery

Samson had an overindulgence for women and rebelliousness. Delilah, his lover, was not the only woman that enticed Samson's interest. Delilah was loyal to her kinsmen and demonstrated disloyalty toward Samson. Delilah was offered eleven hundred pieces of silver from multiple kinsmen to find the secret of Samson's strength. The story reads that Delilah was persistent about her evil quest. She pestered, pressed, and vexed Samson's soul to death every day until he told her where the secret lied. Samson told Delilah everything, where his strength lay, that his strength was from God, and it was to be used for God. After she found the secret to his strength, she tormented him even more. She was paid her just reward. Samson's hair was shaved, and God's strength left him. Delilah's kinsmen rejoiced over Samson's disclosure. They bound him, put his eyes out, and imprisoned him.

Samson was the entertainment during the celebration of his capture. The kinsmen thought God had abandoned Him, even though He departed from Him. But God allowed Samson's hair to return, and God returned to Samson once he humbled himself, asking for God's assistance for the revenge of the removal of his eyes. The request to God was to grant him strength one more time, allowing him to kill those at the celebration, even at the expense of his own life. Samson pulled the pillars of the stadium down with all his might, destroying the people and himself.

Samson was born for purpose, as each of us. Samson's parents were informed by an angel of the Lord that he was to deliver his people out of captivity. Samson had been rebellious in his youth, and this behavior led to pridefulness. Samson was also conceited. He showed off his strength and did not use it in honorable situations. He gained selfish attention instead of being focused on purpose and direction. We also become the adversary entertainment in our rebelliousness and selfishness. We imprison ourselves to the convictions of our vices because they give us immediate pleasure at the expense of ourselves and others. The adversary is persistent in his manner of torment and mockery through pestering our thoughts, making you feel pressed all the time and vexed irritability toward others, especially loved ones, when we are walking in a path of disarray. Can we make our ReCoVery process an influential experience of purpose? Jesus and His disciples offered life changing experiences of deliverance out of captivity to the world. Likewise, we were created to change the world. We are change agents with a catalytic spirit to ignite and arouse flames of enthusiasm, energy, and motivation just like Jesus and His disciples.

-*-Let's Reason Together -*-
_____

I've tried everything, and nothing helps. Now I'm at the end of my rope.

> "He is pure, and everyone who has this hope in him keeps themselves pure like Christ."
> —1 John 3:3 (ERV)

ReCoVery

Let's Reason in Our Thoughts for a Moment...God will perfect those things that concern you.

Are there any concerns understanding that the gratifications of immediate pleasures are costly if not managed?

❧   What is the situation?

❧   What are the circumstances?

❧   What is the relationship?

❧   ReCoVery - Let's get started to Rebuild.

•   Rebuild-

•   Rebuild together-

•   Rebuild in truth-

ReCoVery8

~ Authentic ~

We can call on the Names of God Because our Father attests that
He is our Ever-Present Help. God is our All in All in every Challenge.
Below is a Name of God in Hebrew and the meaning.
We have access to call upon when in need.

Who is God to me Today. . .

Jehovah Jireh ~
The Lord will Provide

ReCoVery

Romans Chapter 8

Meanwhile, the moment we get tired in the waiting, God's Spirit is right alongside helping us along. If we don't know how or what to pray, it doesn't matter. He does our praying in and for us, making prayer out of our wordless sighs, our aching groans. He knows us far better than we know ourselves, knows our pregnant condition, and keeps us present before God. That's why we can be so sure that every detail in our lives of love for God is worked into something good. God knew what he was doing from the very beginning. He decided from the outset to shape the lives of those who love him along the same lines as the life of his Son. The Son stands first in the line of humanity he restored. We see the original and intended shape of our lives there in him. After God made that decision of what his children should be like, he followed it up by calling people by name. After he called them by name, he set them on a solid basis with himself. And then, after getting them established, he stayed with them to the end, gloriously completing what he had begun.

—Romans 8:26–30 (MSG)

ReCoVery

There must be a transition from carnality to authentic Christianity. You may be able to fake a relationship with humanity, but this is not feasible with Jesus Christ. Carnality is immediately associated with our selfish, sometimes secretive, appetites and desires. It is the practice of satisfying our bodily passions.

We are engaged in a lifelong pursuit of practice from the moment we are born. We practice walking, talking, learning alphabets, making words, reading, and writing. The more we practice perfectly, the closer we get to perfecting the skill we are practicing. How long does a doctor or lawyer usually practice medicine? Most of the time, it's usually a lifelong endeavor of appreciating their chosen profession or professional commitment, serving in their practice, confronting the challenges of their profession, and pressing onward as their profession evolves over time. We too can appreciate a committed practice of service to Jesus Christ while confronting our challenges as we grow and evolve over time as a Christ follower. We should have victory in this life as we grow in practicing Christlikeness because the grace of God is sufficient. It's enough when we feel weak. When we feel lifeless without the strength to do, that's when Christ becomes our power.

God has all authority, just like we have all authority in our desires. We choose what pleases us. That is what God does. He chooses what pleases Him, and He hopes that you would desire to please Him. Humanity is God's greatest endeavor. When God created us, He said it was good. Developing a prayer life helps you develop spiritual insight into the way of pleasing and honoring Christ as Lord over our lives. As we move from carnality to authenticity, we are to see growth in our Christian development. This is like evidence of personal and professional development. As we practice the right things pertaining to what we desire to develop, it will be displayed in our actions and skillset performance. These areas are enhanced, and the manifestation of growth will be evident outwardly. As an analogy, an apple tree will produce apples. A Christian produces Christlike character, which is love, joy, peace, patience, kindness, goodness, faithfulness, gentleness, and self-control. As we continue to grow in Christlikeness, our thoughts become Christlike, catering more to His will for our lives versus our will for our lives.

-*-Let's Reason Together -*-

Our thoughts are not like Christ's thoughts. We only know in part. 1 Corinthians 13:9–10 (NLT) reads, "now our knowledge is partial and incomplete ..." But unfortunately our choices have lasting effects even though our decisions are based on partial intellectual reasoning. We remain responsible for our situations, circumstances, and relationships.

> "You are our hope, our joy, and the crown we will be
> proud of when our Lord Jesus Christ comes."
> —1 Thessalonians 2:19 (ERV)

ReCoVery

Most of us know the infamous Bible truth of King David and Goliath. King David killed Goliath, the Philistine, with a slingshot to his head and beheaded him with his sword. King David was known as a warrior for his kingdom and a man after God's own heart. But most people may not know that King David was also a murderer and an adulterer. Yet he was a man who pleased God. Once confronted for his wrongdoings, he decided that he would self-evaluate his actions. King David asked God for forgiveness with a repentant heart for his wrong behaviors, thoughts, and deeds daily. Before King David routinely talked with God in prayer, he intentionally purposed to repent, just in case his heart decisions were not right with God.

One day while King David was taking a day off from war and relaxing, he saw something pleasing to his eyes. He decided to take it because he was the king. This decision cost King David the life of a loyal soldier named Uriah, whom he murdered. King David was engaged in an adulterous affair with Uriah's wife after desiring her from afar. His decision also cost him the life of his newborn child, an accomplice to his son's death, and life experiences of many oppositional family crises, especially with his children.

The true Word of God reads that the adversary accuses each of us to God day and night, seeking a verdict of guilty and shame from those claims. He discusses and disputes over our behavior, pointing the finger at our doings. It is written in the book of Proverbs that even a child is known by their doings. The adversary thinks in case God doesn't know what we've been doing, he will maliciously expose us to the Father, yet he doesn't like to be exposed.

We have the same right, authority, and jurisdiction as well. We have the legal right to approach the throne of grace for mercy to reverse the accusations, disputed issues, and overthrow the verdict of the accuser. As we communicate and spend intimate time with the Father in prayer, we are entering His courtroom. In prayer, we are interceding on our own behalf and standing to defend ourselves. Our requests are in conjunction with the intercessions that Christ Jesus makes to the Father. The takings of prayer have an interception effect on the accusations preventing the adversary victory. Retrospectively we get the victory.

-*-Let's Reason Together -*-
_____

Jesus Christ's forgiveness is for all. Christ forgives the rapist, robber, murderer, drug dealer selling drugs to your school-age child, prostitute, husband or wife engaged in an adulteress affair, child that lies to his parents, wife beaten by her husband, pedophile, and so forth. We have all unfortunately sinned and fallen short.

> "And so, Lord, my only hope is in you."
>
> —Psalm 39:7 (TLB)

ReCoVery

King David was also known as a psalmist, a composer of music. He is the author of many chapters in the book of Psalms. The message of the Psalms is so very beautiful ranging from prayers and questioning God's actions to praising God's actions in worship and exaltations. The Psalms offers prayers of thanksgiving to our Savior and prayers of warfare against the adversary.

King David wrote the psalms because he often felt alone, isolated, forsaken, broken, used, unworthy, and envied by many of his enemies wanting to kill him. In addition to all the challenges of being a parent and a king, he cried out for supernatural assistance from God, just like most of us do when we become overwhelmed with life. Our God is a hearing God. He hears us and will answer us (Psalm 91:15; Jeremiah 33:3; Isaiah 65:24). Our personal testimonies and the biblical stories both witness the truth about our Lord Jesus Christ over and over.

ReCoVery

<u>Let's Reason in Our Thoughts for a Moment</u>...God will perfect those things that concern you.

Are there any concerns understanding the need to establish authenticity in Christ Jesus?

❖ What is the situation?

❖ What are the circumstances?

❖ What is the relationship?

❖ ReCoVery ~ Let's get started to Rebuild.

- Rebuild~

- Rebuild Together~

- Rebuild In truth~

ReCoVery

Everything Has Its Time

To every thing there is a season,
A time for every purpose under heaven:
A time to be born,
And a time to die;
A time to plant,
And a time to pluck what is planted;
A time to kill,
And a time to heal;
A time to break down,
And a time to build up;
A time to weep,
And a time to laugh;
A time to mourn,
And a time to dance;
A time to cast away stones,
And a time to gather stones;
A time to embrace,
And a time to refrain from embracing;
A time to gain,
And a time to lose;
A time to keep,
And a time to throw away;
A time to tear,
And a time to sew;
A time to keep silence,
And a time to speak;
A time to love,
And a time to hate;
A time of war,
And a time of peace.
Ecclesiastes 3:1–8 (NKJV)

Part Three

~ All the Days of My Life~

ReCoVery9

~ Death & Dying ~

We can call on the Names of God Because our Father attests that
He is our Ever-Present Help. God is our All in All in every Challenge.
Below is a Name of God in Hebrew and the meaning.
We have access to call upon when in need.

Who is God to me Today...

Jehovah Shalom ~ The Lord Is Peace

ReCoVery

Romans Chapter 9

Is that grounds for complaining that God is unfair? Not so fast, please. God told Moses, "I'm in charge of mercy. I'm in charge of compassion." Compassion doesn't originate in our bleeding hearts or moral sweat, but in God's mercy. The same point was made when God said to Pharaoh, "I picked you as a bit player in this drama of my salvation power." All we're saying is that God has the first word, initiating the action in which we play our part for good or ill.

—Romans 9:14–18 (MSG)

ReCoVery

With great regards, my beloved, I honestly felt inspired to share this topic. Death and dying is a sensitive place in our lives for all of humanity. This is predominately because living beings only know life. We are alive! No matter how challenging life may seem, that is all we have experienced, and that is what we desire. The word of truth attests that in our present state of mind, we only know in part intellectually based on God's omnipotence, who knows all things. Therefore, we may not have all the answers, but we do know that we are all in this together in unity or discord.

Life is for the living. It is the living that cares for the death and dying. It is only the living that can ReCoVery from the loss of their loved ones. Our family members would want us to go forward in this life, and only the living can stand to rectify a possible thought of an untimely cause of death. As we place Christ Jesus as the centerpiece of our heart, we will experience ReCoVery. Christ removed the sting of death from the dying, but He has not removed the sting of life from the living.

The September 11, 2001 (9-11) mass destruction of the World Trade Center in New York City remains afresh in my thoughts. The entire situation and surrounding circumstantial plot were the epitome of evil. This was the most hideous event many Americans ever experienced on their homeland.

Humanity and most living things are resilient when it comes to life, I believe, mainly because there are so many of us in the world with such a beautiful array of versatility. The versatility becomes like adrenaline. Humanity overwhelmingly experiences a sudden rush of adrenaline to confront the attack with personal and professional passion, utilizing whatever they must to help rectify the situation immediately.

The actions taken by the trapped individuals were horrendously sorrowful, and the loss of the many first responders—firefighters, police officers, and paramedics—was terribly sad. Unfortunately, life presentations are not always what we would like them to be. We humankind all share the horror of the moment—the good, the bad, and the ugly alike.

-*-Let's Reason Together -*-

Then they cried out to the Lord in their trouble, and He saved them out of their distresses. He brought them out of darkness and the shadow of death and broke their chains in pieces.

- *Oh, that men would give thanks to the Lord for His goodness, and for His wonderful works to the children of men!* (Psalms 107:13-15 NKJV)

"Love never gives up on people. It never stops trusting, never loses hope, and never quits."
—1 Corinthians 13:7 (ERV)

ReCoVery

God orchestrates His divine grace on our behalf because of His great goodness and mercy that follows us all the days of our lives. His mercy will never end, they are renewed each morning, and more importantly, Christ Jesus faithfully loves each of us. He has faith in us, and He is faithful to us. Our Father will take care of all presented problems because He is our ever-present help. It may look like it's the end, but we keep going in faith.

Sometimes there are no words to describe the calamitous horror of the moment felt by humans. As a registered nurse, I have experienced both death and dying of my personal family members as well as family members that I'm obligated to care for in health care. This deeply sad occasion warrants love and mercy with an offering of condolences. Naturally, it is a time to support the relatives to grieve the best they know how. The affairs of life affect each of us uniquely different. Catastrophic events are often a prelude to the unity of humanity, and we become harmoniously one for the cause.

Moreover, when trapped in an unpleasant situation, we may find it challenging and necessary to resort to a new, innovative way of claiming up out of the pit. My son, Yuri Stephon, was challenged by his mentor to create something positive from the unfortunate 9-11 event. He came up with an ingenious idea and created a motivational platform called 911 DreamBuilders. The 911 DreamBuilders is a speaking platform that poses an offering of encouragement to always dream. The platform addresses the desire to build upon the many dreams that were lost and destroyed. Now they will live through others.

The Coronavirus Disease 2019 (COVID-19) has fiercely exploded on the scene of our lives with a vengeance. The roar of COVID-19 is undeniable and has gripped the entire world to succumb to a deadly fear. The adversary is a deceiver of the whole world, utilizing methods of deep afflictions, suffering, pain, and sorrow. However, like myself and others who have survived COVID-19, we have ReCoVery of life. Thank You, Jesus!

-*-Let's Reason Together -*-

Then they cried out to the Lord in their trouble, and He saved them out of their distresses. He sent His word and healed them and delivered them from their destruction.

- *Oh, that men would give thanks to the Lord for His goodness, and for His wonderful works to the children of men!* (Psalm 107:19–21 NKJV).

> "I would have been without hope if I had not believed that I would see the loving-kindness of the Lord in the land of the living."
>
> —Psalm 27:13 (NLV)

ReCoVery

The challenge about anything when it is new, humanity never believes that they would be the one that would get the sting of it. COVID-19 is not new, pandemics are not new, humanity is not new, and the word of Christ Jesus is not new, unlike 9-11, which appeared like an irredeemable situation. Many family members had no opportunity for closure because the trapped victims felt hopeless. On the other hand, COVID-19 victims experienced a range of signs and symptoms over time from mild to lifelessness, yet there is still no comfort despite the time factor.

The truthful, infallible Word of God records that Christ Jesus removed the sting from death at the cross and on resurrection day. The Bible records that our King Jesus Christ has conquered the last enemy, which is death (1 Corinthians 15:26 NKJV). While many would say that doesn't negate the fact that they have lost family members. Yes, that is correct, and that statement is understandable. As a Bible believer of the good news, I've positioned myself to believe that the Holy Bible features the salvation of Jesus Christ while offering hope ("helping other people eternally") that is obtainable with joy ("just one yes to Jesus").

The biblical truth in the book of Revelation reads that one day there will be no more tears, no more death, no more mourning, no more crying, and no more pain and that all things now visible will be no more. In addition, it is appointed to all of humanity the same destination the receiving of judgment upon Jesus's return. Understandably, we only desire life in this life, and death is not something we desire to become accustomed to.

The peace that comes from Christ that surpasses all understanding may offer us the courage and comfort to confront death and dying. The true Word of God reads in Luke 2:14 (NCV), "Glory to our Father in heaven and earth peace to the people who pleases God." The people who please God are the people who accept Him as Savior. We can better recover from our loss of loved ones in Christ Jesus when we have a personal relationship with the Father as He becomes our All in All in this life.

~⁺~Let's Reason Together ~*~

_____

Then they cry out to the Lord in their trouble, and He brings them out of their distresses. He calms the storm, so that its waves are still. Then they are glad because they are quiet; So, He guides them to their desired haven.

- *Oh, that men would give thanks to the Lord for His goodness, and for His wonderful works to the children of men!* (Psalm 107:28–31 NKJV).

> "I say this because I know the plans that I have for you. This
> message is from the LORD. I have good plans for you. I don't plan
> to hurt you. I plan to give you hope and a good future."
>
> —Jeremiah 29:11 (ERV)

ReCoVery

Let's Reason in Our Thoughts for a Moment...God will perfect those things that concern you.

Are there any concerns understanding the importance that the living can experience ReCoVery.

❖   What is the situation?

❖   What are the circumstances?

❖   What is the relationship?

❖   ReCoVery ~ Let's get started to Rebuild.

•   Rebuild~

•   Rebuild together~

•   Rebuild in truth~

ReCoVery10

~ Father ~

ReCoVery

We can call on the Names of God Because our Father attests that
He is our Ever-Present Help. God is our All in All in every Challenge.
Below is a Name of God in Hebrew and the meaning.
We have access to call upon when in need.

Who is God to me Today…

Jehovah Rapha ~ The Lord That Heals

ReCoVery

Romans Chapter 10

Scripture reassures us, "No one who trusts God like this—heart and soul—will ever regret it." It's exactly the same no matter what a person's religious background may be: the same God for all of us, acting the same incredibly generous way to everyone who calls out for help. "Everyone who calls, 'Help, God!' gets help." But how can people call for help if they don't know who to trust? And how can they know who to trust if they haven't heard of the One who can be trusted? And how can they hear if nobody tells them? And how is anyone going to tell them, unless someone is sent to do it? That's why Scripture exclaims, A sight to take your breath away! Grand processions of people telling all the good things of God! But not everybody is ready for this, ready to see and hear and act. Isaiah asked what we all ask at one time or another: "Does anyone care, God? Is anyone listening and believing a word of it?" The point is: Before you trust, you have to listen. But unless Christ's Word is preached, there's nothing to listen to.

—Romans 10:11–17 (MSG)

ReCoVery

Fathers are sort of "thy kingdom come" to each family. It was Christ who elected fathers to be the facsimile of Himself. Fathers are the closest species on earth that replicates the position of our Father in heaven. It is hugely significant that a male was the first created living organism of mankind in God's image. This is a most honored position on all the earth. It has a profound status of critical importance to the individual, family, and community. We know that there is the intellectual image because God verbally communicated with man first, giving him instructions, and he was able to respond to the instructions with intellectual comprehension.

The father is often the first-sent help in many family matters. It is not a coincidence that fatherless homes have increased, and the many reasons are unlimited. God the Father's relationship with the church is modeled after the union of marriage. Each saved individual is the church. People are the synagogue because Jesus Christ now lives in us. We humanity are the living temple. The church building is where we congregate, and the building is nothing without the people. In God's family of mankind, Christ created the father to be positioned as head of the household. There is a question on the income tax form that asks who the head of household is. Due to the destruction of the family, this is an unfortunate question to ask sometimes. The era in which we live, the head of the household may unfortunately vary from a fourteen-year-old unwed mother to a ninety-year-old great-grandmother. Fathers being the head of the household? Can this ordained position be recovered? It is God's grace and purpose in choosing men to be fathers as well as women to be mothers. These positions are the glory of mankind.

Children need the male dominance of a father for discipline. Fathers are to teach their sons to serve, respect, and honor the female images within the home, mothers and sisters. This is how the sons would learn to treat their wives. Women are more often physiologically hurt by men because many male seeds are without fatherly examples. Usually sons commit to what they see their fathers do. Jesus Christ is the great Abba Father. He is our example when we do not have a good example. Unfortunately a mother cannot be the family role model of a father, but this is prevalent today. This was not the plan for the kingdom of God. The first thing Christians become are disciples to learn discipline of becoming a Christ follower. Christians are discipled by their Father through His word. The Bible teaches and supports the belief that fathers are to teach the word of God to their children, walking and talking daily upon awakening and going to sleep. The words are to become meshed into their hearts, souls, and spirit. But if the father doesn't have it in their hearts, what do we do? We have a mediator called Abba Father, Jesus Christ of all creation.

-*-Let's Reason Together -*-

Our Father the Creator does not desire what He created, worshipping what He Himself created.

"What good people hope for brings happiness, but what the wicked hope for brings destruction."

—Proverb 10:28 (ERV)

94

ReCoVery

Society has selected to honor fathers and mothers one day out of the year, but the true word of God connects the honor to a promise of long life. Like love and forgiveness, fathers and mothers are the powerhouses of life. God, the creator of all things, would not give a father the assigned position to take care of the family in harmony without a care plan. Fathers are royal priests for the household. He is kingship, the head of household with priestly duties of mediator between Christ and man, his family members. The father is the gap stander of the family.

The male seed has the ordained position to assign the sex of each child, and each of the children is birthed through the womb of a female seed. This process is the same throughout all of creation, which Christ designed. The biblical truth of Job 1 beautifully highlights the father's role in the family. It reads that Job routinely stood in the gap by communicating with God on behalf of his children. Job did this just in case his children made the heart decision to engage in wrongdoings and curse God. Job's communications intercepted possible negative outcomes before they happened because Job stood in the gab daily and consistently for his family matters. Who is behind the sabotage of robbing the family of fathers, fathers of fatherhood, and royal priest of their priestly duties? The adversary.

The father is the priestly ambassador mediator between God and man. In the religion of Catholicism, the priest is called "Father." He is the mediator of family matters during the congregation of mass between God and man. When we know our position in war, we are closest to winning. The father position is a warring position for humanity, the sanctity of life. Originally, only men went to the battlefield to fight.

The plight of the family is a battle cry. Our commander-in-chief and spiritual father charges us as military dignitaries for the world to fight victoriously with our full armor intact for our family, sons, daughters, wives, and husbands. We are to be strong in the power of the might of Jesus Christ.

Why did God give fathers the determining factor of the sex of the child? The father was created first in the image of God. Our heavenly Father has the power to create everything; therefore, He created male and female. Earthly fathers, like their heavenly Father, are the only ones who have the exact power to also create male and female. Faith and obedience are the hallmarks of Christianity. There is much technology in the world today, but to date, there remains to be only one way to reproduce. God's way - through the reproduction cells of a male and female.

-*-Let's Reason Together -*-

He is one God and Father of all.

> "For You, O Lord, are my hope, my trust, O LORD, from my youth."
>
> —Psalm 71:5 (ESV)

ReCoVery

Let's Reason in Our Thoughts for a Moment...God will perfect those things that concern you.

Are there any concerns understanding the importance of the father in the family?

❖   What is the situation?

❖   What are the circumstances?

❖   What is the relationship?

❖   ReCoVery ~ Let's get started to Rebuild.

•   Rebuild~

•   Rebuild together~

•   Rebuild in truth~

ReCoVery11

~ Mother ~

We can call on the Names of God Because our Father attests that
He is our Ever-Present Help. God is our All in All in every Challenge.
Below is a Name of God in Hebrew and the meaning.
We have access to call upon when in need.

Who is God to me Today...

El Qanna ~ Jealous God

ReCoVery

Romans Chapter 11

Have you ever come on anything quite like this extravagant generosity of God, this deep, deep wisdom? It's way over our heads. We'll never figure it out. Is there anyone around who can explain God? Anyone smart enough to tell him what to do? Anyone who has done him such a huge favor that God has to ask his advice? Everything comes from him; Everything happens through him; Everything ends up in Him. Always glory! Always praise! Yes. Yes. Yes.

—Romans 11:33–36 (MSG)

ReCoVery

Christ Jesus, my Father, has blessed me with a ministry called "Mothers In Prayer For Their Sons Inc." The ministry of ReCoVery and Mothers In Prayer For Their Sons are both housed at the Ambassador Pavilion, for Christians are ambassadors for Christ, pleading hearers to respond to the message of the good news.

Mothers In Prayer For Their Sons was forthcoming by what I saw when I was a little girl. One early evening when I was a young girl in elementary school, my brother, who was the oldest, was in front of the neighborhood store with a group of his friends. Unbeknownst to me, I have remembered this vision all my life, replaying in my mind at random. We lived on the second floor of a two-story house. My mother had the living room window raised upward as high as it could reach with her body halfway hanging outside the window. The position she was in would not have taken much for her to literally fall out the window. It appeared that her purpose to gain his attention was quite intense.

I remembered my mother calling out loud. She yelled and screamed his name, telling him to come upstairs, now repetitively until he responded. There must have been something not right going on outside amongst my brother and his friends that made my mother call him home. My mother was a woman who followed her motherly intuition. She always knew when something was going on with each of her children. Most mothers have something special in their hearts for the safety and protection of their children. I believe that moment made me look at the love, care, and welfare my mother cherished for my brother. My sister and I often thought in the back of our minds that she favored our brother. Somehow, this incident brought the thought closer to the forefront of my mind.

As I grew older and birthed two sons of my own, I realized what my mother had accomplished on that day. I also realized that it was not that my mother favored my brother, but it was something much deeper and more disturbing, and I now understood that vision that replayed in my mind throughout a lifetime. My mother's intuition protected and saved my brother's life at that very moment.

-*-Let's Reason Together -*-

If we as humans knew the full essence of what we do to ourselves and one another, we would not do it. But we don't know. That's why we often do anything to ourselves without genuinely thinking about the outcome.

> "We are so sure of this hope that we can speak very openly."
> —2 Corinthians 3:12 (ERV)

ReCoVery

Later in life, I learned that my brother and his friends were planning to do something not right that night, and my mother intercepted their plans and prevented an ugly situation from happening. Mothers save the lives of their sons. My mother not only saved her son's life but the lives of the other sons. This is a biblical and futuristic occurrence that mothers are often involved in the destination of their son.

Let's review the Bible truth surrounding the circumstances of how Moses' mother saved his life. Pharaoh, the Egyptian king, was afraid that the enslaved Hebrew people would possibly join forces with his enemies and war against him. In war, when an enemy wanted to destroy a people, they would destroy (kill) the male seed. Pharaoh gave orders to the midwives who were delivering Hebrew babies to kill all baby boys at birth but allow the baby girls to live. Pharaoh also commanded the Egyptian people to kill all Hebrew boys that were born in the vicinity. They were to kill them and throw them into the Nile River.

Moses' biological mother hid her pregnancy from Pharaoh for three months. She gave birth to her son and placed him in a basket, sending him into a dangerous river of waters in hope that her actions would save her son's life. At that point, she had done all she could humanly to protect her son. With Jesus Christ, all things are possible, and He will always send help for your concern. How did Moses' mother recover from the loss of her child floating down the river? While taking a bath in the Nile River, Pharaoh's daughter found the Hebrew baby floating down the Nile. She took the child to safety and sought to find someone to nurse the child.

Moses' mother had sent his older sibling to follow the floating basket, and Moses' sister heard the conversation of needing a nurse for the baby. Moses' sister offered Moses' mother for the job and received a salary for nursing her own son. Moses was returned to his biological mother to be nursed, and the two mothers shared love for the one child. Pharaoh's daughter did not know that Moses was nursed by his very own biological mother.

Moses' adopted mother saved his life by allowing him to grow as a free Egyptian. Moses' adopted mother was the daughter of Pharaoh, the king of Egypt. Moses' biological mother sent him down the Nile, and his adopted mother received and recovered the precious treasure and raised him into royalty.

-*-Let's Reason Together -*-
_____

Later in life I learned …

"The hope of the righteous people leads to joy …"
—Proverbs 10:28 (GW)

ReCoVery

Both my mother and Moses' mother did all they could do humanly at the immediate moment to save their sons' lives and destinations. I have always had a heart of a caretaker for the male seed, and I know why I have a love and passion for them. Christ has given me a heartfelt passion in my heart that drives me to pray for the male seed. I have since established the intercessory ministry of Mothers In Prayer For Their Sons. I have hopeful dreams of an international prayer march for sons at the Washington Monument, the joining of mothers across the world united in one location, praying to Abba Father of heaven and earth on behalf of male seeds—sons, husbands, uncles, nephews, neighbors, and friends.

Again, this has been a vision in the back of my mind all my life. Christ called and ordained the female to be the male's help meet. Wives are their husband's helpmate, and mothers are their son's helpmate. We help them meet their ordained calling for purpose. God made each mother suitable for their son as well as each wife suitable for their husband. It is not often you hear of a mother giving up on her son, no matter how challenging, and wives are most often the last to give up on the marriage. I believe by design, females usually keep hope alive in most situations, circumstances, and relationships.

When I see my sons engaged in something that purposes success, I hope success for them and all sons. I had homeschooled my sons with their male cousins, encouraging them to collaborate during study time. My sons were active in playing instruments, and I sought out the same instructions for my nephew. I had paid for a male tutor to not just tutor my sons to be successful in taking the high school scholastic achievement test, but I've paid for the entire football team that they were a part of to be tutored for success as well.

As my mother saved the life of her son, she also saved the lives of my brother's friends. The ministry of Mothers In Prayer For Their Sons came into fruition one day while praying for my sons. I worked at a facility that cared for young males. I thought as I looked at them outside of my office window, "Their mothers would want me to pray for them too."

I started praying for them every day when I prayed for my sons. Of all the many places of employment as a registered nurse, it was one of my most favorable work environments. Moses' mother and my mother decided to take a stance by taking the proactive route, intercepting many negative possibilities in the lives of their sons.

-*-Let's Reason Together -*-

Both my mother and Moses' mother did all they could do humanly at that immediate moment to save their sons' lives and destinations.

> "My soul can say, 'The Lord is my lot in life. That is why I find hope in Him.'"
>
> —Lamentation 3:24 (GW)

ReCoVery

To share another mother-related story, it is a frightening experience to receive a phone call at three in the morning from a hospital about your child. My eldest son, Larry Randal, went to a fraternity party in his senior year of high school, where one of the guests shot him. He told the story that he was dancing and stepped on the toes of a guy at the party. Throughout the remainder of the party, the guy followed and threatened him by showing my son his gun from under his clothing. At the end of the party, Larry tried to exit through another door before being seen by the guy, but his efforts failed

The young man continued to harass my son and waited for him outside, despite his efforts to prevent being engaged in this troublesome situation. Unfortunately he shot my son. Larry was hospitalized in the emergency department when we received the call. He was cared for and ready for release by the time I arrived. Larry was on the mend of healing physiologically, but psychologically, he was challenged by the overall experience.

My son Larry was scheduled to run a track meet at school. He wasn't sure if he were ready for the challenge because he was healing and still experiencing some pain from the injury site. He asked my advice if he should run or not. He had the position of being the anchor leg in the relay race. I told him that he would make the final decision. I challenged him to the challenge, informing him that the enemy's number-one position in our lives is to steal our victory, destroy our purpose, and kill any possible hope of anything from us by any means necessary. I suggested that we could coordinate pain management just prior to the race and it would be effective when he most needed it after the race. He agreed with the plan and ran the anchor in the relay. Of course it was a proud moment for him in spite of his earlier loss.

The quest for life is always in the challenge. My son lived to recover from the injury and recovered from the challenge of running the race not fully healed, and the ReCoVery process gave him a life testimony that our King Jesus will never leave you or forsake you.

-*-Let's Reason Together -*-
_____

Our sons need our daily prayers, and as mothers, we should always desire to keep hope alive! We must pray daily for an assigned anointing to destroy the work of the devil and believe that in Christ Jesus we are victorious in prevailing.

> "For surely there is a latter end [a future and a reward], and
> your hope and expectation shall not be cut off."
>
> —Proverbs 23:18 (AMPC)

ReCoVery

Let's Reason in Our Thoughts for a Moment... God will perfect those things that concern you.

Are there any concerns understanding the importance of the Mother in the family?

❖   What is the situation?

❖   What are the circumstances?

❖   What is the relationship?

❖   ReCoVery ~ Let's get started to Rebuild.

•   Rebuild~

•   Rebuild together~

•   Rebuild in truth~

ReCoVery12

ReCoVery

~ Angel ~

We can call on the Names of God Because our Father attests that
He is our Ever-Present Help. God is our All in All in every Challenge.
Below is a Name of God in Hebrew and the meaning.
We have access to call upon when in need.

Who is God to me Today...

Jehovah Nissi ~
The Lord My Banner

ReCoVery

Romans Chapter 12

So here's what I want you to do, God helping you: Take your everyday, ordinary life—your sleeping, eating, going-to-work, and walking-around life—and place it before God as an offering. Embracing what God does for you is the best thing you can do for him. Don't become so well-adjusted to your culture that you fit into it without even thinking. Instead, fix your attention on God. You'll be changed from the inside out. Readily recognize what he wants from you, and quickly respond to it. Unlike the culture around you, always dragging you down to its level of immaturity, God brings the best out of you, develops well-formed maturity in you.

I'm speaking to you out of deep gratitude for all that God has given me, and especially as I have responsibilities in relation to you. Living then, as every one of you does, in pure grace, it's important that you not misinterpret yourselves as people who are bringing this goodness to God. No, God brings it all to you. The only accurate way to understand ourselves is by what God is and by what he does for us, not by what we are and what we do for him.

—Romans 12:1–3 (MSG)

ReCoVery

I remember when in my addiction and while in a drunken stupor, I was trying to get home in the middle of the night on the A train in Brooklyn, New York. It may have been two or three in the morning. I don't remember where I was coming from because the A train was not on the immediate train line that I lived. I would have to transfer to another line to reach my home by the subway system.

I was very sleepy, and I was having difficulties staying awake during the train ride. The complete A train ride from one end of the line to the start over thirty miles, a two-hour ride one way. The A train is the longest subway line in the entire subway system. The train ride from Far Rockaways includes the Jamaica Bay Bridge, which extends three thousand feet long. The body of water is so awfully close beneath the train that it seems as though you are taking a boat ride excursion. When you look out the train window, there is nothing but water all around. The trip spans through the Aqueduct Racetrack in Brooklyn, John F. Kennedy International Airport (JFK) in Queens, Port Authority Bus Terminal, Museum of Natural History, and Harlem. All three of these locations are in New York City, and the train reaches the last stop of the line at Inwood, New York.

I was on the A train all night, riding back and forth, passing my train stop over and over again. Late into the night to early morning, there are fewer people on the trains. Often it is believed that the more people on the train, the safer the ride. It is also somewhat safer to ride in the car near the train conductor who opens and closes the train car doors. Now let's picture this escapade traveling on the subway at three in the morning, asleep and alone, no one in the train car to assist or protect me, and I was not seated in the conductor car. I was a defenseless prey for the criminal-minded night stalkers, thieves, and rapists.

I woke up suddenly realizing what was happening, jumped up, and got off the train. I did not pay attention to the subway stop. I just got off. This stop was called Broadway Junction in Brooklyn. It was dark with poor lighting, isolated, and without people traffic in the middle of the night. The East New York Train Track Yard and the East New York Bus Hub housed both Mass Transit Authority (MTA) parked unused trains and buses until the need arose for operation. The area was saturated with connecting train tracks on the ground and high overhead train tracks in the sky, empty trains, and empty buses. The area had scattered trees, personal and abandoned parked cars, and debris throughout the grounds.

-*-Let's Reason Together -*-
_____

All that are in Heaven and Earth are His servants! THE CREATOR.

> "May your faithful love rest on us, LORD, for we put our hope in your."
> —Psalms 33:22 (CSB)

ReCoVery

The *New York Daily News* reported that Broadway Junction has either the highest or among the highest boroughwide rates of misdemeanor sex crimes (19), violent crimes (113), property crimes (152), drug crimes (28), and weapons possession charges (320). I also passed another unsafe train stop going toward the Rockaways called Broad Channel. The *New York Daily News* reported that Broad Channel was the most dangerous station in New York City, where there were 27.38 crimes per 100,000 riders.[8]

Another area of semi-safety is near the MTA train booth. This is where you would purchase the subway fare. People stand near this area after going through the subway turnstiles close to the train platform. Finally, I passed my last area of safety and entered the street of the isolated train yard and bus depot. I was out of my human mind.

As I exited the door directly in front of the train station, there came a taxi out of nowhere. I didn't think or question. I just got into the taxi and told the driver my address. I lived approximately seven miles, and I was oblivious of the whole taxi trip to my apartment. Again, I fell asleep and did not awaken until the taxi driver arrived at my apartment, came around to my car door, woke me up, took me out of the car, and escorted me to my third-floor apartment. I remembered that I even gave him the keys to open both the lobby and apartment doors. He accompanied me into my apartment, gave me my house keys, and left the apartment, all uneventful.

You have of course assessed a deeply foolish crazy young lady in trouble at this point and seriously in need (sin) of Jesus. This is how we assist the adversary in our demise, the transfer of ownership of our lives. I had now become what the adversary desired for my life, dead alive, no good to myself, my family, my community, my country, my world, or the kingdom of God. I was not in control of my life. How do I account for my safe delivery? You may say sheer coincidence. I dare not. I believe it was the grace of God! I believe that my Lord Christ Jesus sent an angel to rescue me to safety, first the rescue and then the ReCoVery. Angels are sent messages of God, and Christ Jesus sent this messenger to rescue and escort me to safety.

-*-Let's Reason Together -*-

We too are sent messengers of the gospel of Christ Jesus, and "I'm lovin' it!"

> "But Happy is the man who has the God of Jacob for his
> helper, whose hope is in the Lord his God"
>
> —Psalm 146:5 (TLB)

ReCoVery

In the true word of God, angels are usually referred to of the masculine gender. The archangel Michael fought Satan in Revelation 12. In the book of Daniel, Gabriel, another angel, was identified as a man in order to carry out the God-assigned task. An angel Gabriel spoke to Joseph and Mary regarding the birth and announced the child to be named Jesus. He also spoke to Zacharias, John the Baptist's father, and announced his name to be John. In the book of Matthew when Jesus was arrested, he stated that he could pray to his Father and He would dispatch twelve legions (one legion equals three thousand to six thousand soldiers) of angels to escort Him to safety.

Christ will always allow for an escort to safety while having the plan of ReCoVery in the workings for you. As a family member of the household of the kingdom of God, I can identify with my adoption rights. I am honored to be a Christian. I'm allowed all privileges as well as the rest of the family who belong to Jesus along with all the patriots of the Bible of the kingdom of God. We all have the same Father. If Jesus says He had access to one legion of angels, I have access to one legion of angels. A Bible truth in 2 Kings is that our Father sent and filled a mountain with angels. It was called chariots of fire to help the prophet Elisha. In the book of Genesis, an angel was sent to Haggar, an Egyptian maid servant of Sarai and concubine of Abraham. The angel provided water and safety during her desperate wandering in a dry desert after she and her son were placed out of their home by Abraham and Sarai.

Can we reflect for a moment how we have so much faith in the substance of choice? We don't know what we are purchasing, and it could be deadly poison. This is when Christ makes us lie down in green pastures. We must be made because our thought process does not allow us to make right decisions for our lives. We can put all our trust in the entire Bible truth of God's word, just like we use to put all of our trust in the substance usage and ReCoVery losses.

-*-Let's Reason Together -*-
_____

We can recover losses.

> "Be strong, all who wait with hope for the Lord, and let your heart be courageous."
> —Psalm 31:24 (GW)

ReCoVery

Let's Reason in Our Thoughts for a Moment…God will perfect those things that concern you.

Are there any concerns understanding the importance of putting all your trust in the complete Gospel like you use to put all your trust in substance usage and ReCoVery all losses?

- ❖ What is the situation?

- ❖ What are the circumstances?

- ❖ What is the relationship?

- ❖ ReCoVery ~ Let's get started to Rebuild.

- • Rebuild~

- • Rebuild together~

- • Rebuild in truth~

ReCoVery

A Dialogue between Jesus, a Man, and the Disciples
Mark 10:17–31 (MSG)

As he went out into the street, a man came running up, greeted him with great reverence, and asked, "Good Teacher, what must I do to get eternal life?"

Jesus said, "Why are you calling me good? No one is good, only God. You know the commandments: Don't murder, don't commit adultery, don't steal, don't lie, don't cheat, honor your father and mother."

The man said, "Teacher, I have from my youth kept them all!"

Jesus looked him hard in the eye—and loved him! He said, "There's one thing left: Go sell whatever you own and give it to the poor. All your wealth will then be heavenly wealth. And come follow me."

The man's face clouded over. This was the last thing he expected to hear, and he walked off with a heavy heart. He was holding on tight to a lot of things, and not about to let go.

Looking at his disciples, Jesus said, "Do you have any idea how difficult it is for people who 'have it all' to enter God's kingdom?" The disciples couldn't believe what they were hearing, but Jesus kept on: "You can't imagine how difficult. I'd say it's easier for a camel to go through a needle's eye than for the rich to get into God's kingdom."

That got the disciples' attention. "Then who has any chance at all?" they asked.

Jesus was blunt: "No chance at all if you think you can pull it off by yourself. Every chance in the world if you let God do it."

Peter tried another angle: "We left everything and followed you."

Jesus said, "Mark my words, no one who sacrifices house, brothers, sisters, mother, father, children, land whatever because of me and the Message will lose out. They'll get it all back, but multiplied many times in homes, brothers, sisters, mothers, children, and land but also in troubles. And then the bonus of eternal life! This is once again the Great Reversal: Many who are first will end up last and the last first."

Part Four

And I Shall Dwell
~ In the House of the Lord ~

ReCoVery13

~ Pride ~

ReCoVery

We can call on the Names of God Because our Father attests that
He is our Ever-Present Help. God is our All in All in every Challenge.
Below is a Name of God in Hebrew and the meaning.
We have access to call upon when in need.

Who is God to me Today...

Jehovah Raah ~
The Lord My Shepherd

ReCoVery

Romans Chapter 13

Don't run up debts, except for the huge debt of love you owe each other. When you love others, you complete what the law has been after all along. The law code—don't sleep with another person's spouse, don't take someone's life, don't take what isn't yours, don't always be wanting what you don't have, and any other "don't" you can think of—finally adds up to this: Love other people as well as you do yourself. You can't go wrong when you love others. When you add up everything in the law code, the sum total is love.

—Romans 13:8–14 (MSG)

ReCoVery

Pride is one of those seven things God hates. We read that there are six things the Lord hates, and the seventh thing is an abomination to Him. They are as follows in the book of Proverbs: pride, lying, hands that shed innocent blood, a heart that devises wicked plans, feet that are swift in running to evil, a false witness who speaks lies, and one who sows discord among the family of Christianity. He hates the seventh even more with disgust because it affects Christian relational fellowship.

Pride allowed Satan to deceive himself. He wanted to be like God. He was thrown out of heaven. There is an order of misfortunate circumstances of a prideful individual: pride comes, then destruction, and finally the fall of the ego.

King Nebuchadnezzar of Babylon (present-day Iraq) was a king in the book of Daniel who fell into this prideful misfortune. He found praise in congratulating himself on his kingdom's accomplishments. He did not praise or acknowledge our God of anything. He believed that he did everything by his own power and majesty. The Most High God, our God, gave King Nebuchadnezzar a dream. The king summoned his wise men, astrologers, fortune-tellers, and magicians to interpret the dream, but they were all unsuccessful. Daniel, a Hebrew captured by the Babylonians, was the only one gifted by our God to interpret the dream. As Daniel understood and explained his interpretation of the dream, it revealed that our God decided to give King Nebuchadnezzar heart and mind as that of a beast. Nebuchadnezzar would no longer think and behave as human, but that of an animal.

This is a most interesting situation that God decided to give the king the heart and mind of a beast in Daniel 4:16–17 (KJV). God did it to prove "that the Most High (God) rules in the kingdom of men …" It is God's ordained determinations that we are and will ever be what He has created us to be. Our creation is not only physiologically and psychologically designed. It is spiritually determined by our creator. We are also defined as a specific kind in our hearts and minds. We are that kind of entity by His definition, having its own distinct existence. A dog will forever function from the specific perspective of its genetic coding deoxyribonucleic acid (DNA) of a dog in heart and a dog in mind.

-*-Let's Reason Together -*-

Can we practice not to do things our God hates?

> "Sustain me according to Your word, that I may live;
> And do not let me be ashamed of my hope."
>
> —Psalm 119:116 (NASB)

ReCoVery

A man or a woman will forever function from the specific perspective of its genetic coding deoxyribonucleic acid (DNA) of a man or a woman in heart and mind by design of our Lord Jesus Christ. Our King Jesus is in the creative nuance of transformation for His glory only. We are to be transformed by a renewed mindset once we become born again, working on acquiring the mind of Christ as we continue to grow in the knowledge of our Lord.

Daniel informed King Nebuchadnezzar of the interpretation of the dream. He would be transformed into an animal for seven years, as the Most High God of all creation ordered. He would live and eat like an animal away from his kingdom. The mercy of God would not take his kingdom from him or keep him in that state of a beast forever. Upon return to his kingdom after he had come to his senses that there is but one God, Nebuchadnezzar would have to come to the revelation knowledge that God is the ruling God of men and God does whatever He pleases. He allows and predetermines life situations, and He does not need our approval or perspective of how to manage the affairs of heaven and earth. Why? We do not always know the answer to that question.

Nebuchadnezzar's nails became like bird's claw, and his body became hairy like eagle's feathers. After seven years, King Nebuchadnezzar returned to his kingdom with a newly refreshed perspective on life that our God is God. Our God is worthy of honor, praise, worship, and glorification. There is none like Him in all heaven and earth. No entity can stop or challenge His royal decree. He can rebirth, transform, and recover those who are prideful, giving them a heart of humility.

-*-Let's Reason Together -*-

King Nebuchadnezzar had an awakening experience! Pridefulness is not an honorable place to be.

> "My soul wait in silence for God alone For my hope is from Him."
> —Psalm 62:5 (NASB)

ReCoVery

<u>Let's Reason in Our thoughts for a Moment</u>... God will perfect those things that concern you

Are there any concerns understanding the six things God hate and that the seventh disgusts Him?

- ❖ What is the situation?

- ❖ What are the circumstances?

- ❖ What is the relationship?

- ❖ ReCoVery - Let's get started to Rebuild.

- • Rebuild-

- • Rebuild together-

- • Rebuild in truth-

ReCoVery14

~ Life ~

We can call on the Names of God Because our Father attests that
He is our Ever-Present Help. God is our All in All in every Challenge.
Below is a Name of God in Hebrew and the meaning.
We have access to call upon when in need.

Who is God to me Today…

Jehovah Sabaoth ~ The Lord of Host

ReCoVery

Romans Chapter 14

Cultivate your own relationship with God, but don't impose it on others. You're fortunate if your behavior and your belief are coherent. But if you're not sure, if you notice that you are acting in ways inconsistent with what you believe—some days trying to impose your opinions on others, other days just trying to please them—then you know that you're out of line. If the way you live isn't consistent with what you believe, then it's wrong.

—Romans 14:22–23 (MSG)

ReCoVery

In our lives, there may be many situations that have a lifeless appearance. This may occur many times because of our selfish and/or self-preservation mindset. It is amazing with all the people in the world, people are the very reason that problems seem like a dead situation. God has created mankind for himself and one another. But are the things in life that we possess ever enough? "No man is an island" is the infamous quotation by John Donne, the seventeenth-century British poet.[9]

Christianity echoes this quotation loud and clear since God not only made mankind, but He also made a ReCoVery way from death to eternal life with Him. We are not an island because we need communal living with others. We need companionship with one another. I appreciate when a stranger greets me with a smile. It brightens my moment, and I give thanksgiving for that person. Community is all around us: online community, neighborhoods, malls, restaurants, grocery stores, and people serving people in our daily exchange outside of our home. When we sell and purchase something, we are serving in the community. Christians serve God by becoming a living sacrifice unto the Father for His will.

The attribute of a mature Christian is to love your neighbor as yourself, which is interesting as you love yourself, you become more selfishly detached to others. Many people love themselves, and they are detached to community engagement. Your neighbor is any human being—your mother, father, children, spouse, friend, enemy, coworker, boss, teacher, and so forth. We get upset about anything, especially things that belong to you (me)!

Recently, I had this overwhelming urge to approach my neighbor and apologize for not being as friendly as I could be. We exchanged some unwanted feelings some time ago. He made an attempt to reconnect, but I did not quite feel the same way at the time. I informed him and his wife that I planned to be a better neighbor because I felt led by the Lord to express the need to apologize. This neighbor moved away shortly after my apology. I was so grateful that I was obedient to Christ's request. I would have felt sad and uneasy if the neighbor had moved and I did not do as Christ asked me. It is necessary to give life to every situation possible.

-*-Let's Reason Together -*-
_____

My heart is hopeful that the word of God is becoming clearer.

> "Is not your fear of God what gives you strength and your good ways that give you hope?"
>
> —Job 4:6 (NLV)

ReCoVery

Life is often not equally fair, but what makes a kind and human statement is when we make a conscious decision to treat others as we would like to be treated. This purposeful decision does not negate the unfairness, but it does allow for a visual or tangible demonstration to another human being that you are concerned and thinking about your own actions toward them. There is a Bible truth in Ezekiel 37 about dead, dry bones coming to life. God took prophet Ezekiel in the spirt to a valley, and within the valley was many dry bones of human remains.

God asked Ezekiel if the dead bones could live. Ezekiel did not say yes or no. He did say that the fate of those bones was in the hands of God. If God wanted them to live, they would, and if he did not, they would not. It was as Jesus said on the cross of Calvary, "Let your will be done." Whatever God is willing for your life will be done.

Christ gave Ezekiel the instructions to speak to the bones. God told Ezekiel to tell the bones to hear the word of the Lord, following the instructions, and he would know that He is Lord God. The spoken word of the Lord was the breath that enters the bones, flesh would come upon the bones, and the bones came alive. All the bones stood up like soldiers as though the area was a war zone of dead soldiers. The bones took on the formation of an army inside the valley. With the miraculous word of Christ, we can speak a thing into existence when we believe. The Bible reads in the book of Hebrews 4:12 that the word of God is alive, active, and powerful!

People are naturally achievers, desiring purpose for their lives. The average person thinks about what they are going to do next all day long. What will be their next inspired goal and how to acquire it? Truthfully speaking, what else is there to do but to accomplish goal after goal? We are naturally born to think and create like our Father. Christ has given mankind so much to choose from in all of life. This versatility makes for all of what's in between the two extremes: rich and poor (an array of poverty to wealth), black and white (an array of beautiful colors in between), up and down (up to the moon and down to the depths of the sea), right and left (as far as to the east as to the west), on and on.

Just like you said to yourself that you were tired of this dead situation of addiction, you were going to get into a ReCoVery program today, and it happened. You spoke it into existence. You spoke what was not present until it became presently real in your life. We have the Christian power and authority to speak a word into our lives, losses, depression, illnesses, poverty, and so forth. Christ will meet us where we believe. We must learn our authority over our lives and speak the word of God into existence for each given situation, circumstance, and relationship expecting a plan of ReCoVery.

-*-Let's Reason Together -*-
_____

Just like you said to yourself that you were tired of your dead situation.

> "Lord, you know the hopes of the helpless. Surely you
> will hear their cries and comfort them."
>
> —Psalm 10:17 (NLT)

ReCoVery

Let's Reason in Our thoughts for a Moment...God will perfect those things that concern you.

Are there any concerns understanding the importance of speaking life into your situation's circumstances, and relationship?

- ❖ What is the situation?

- ❖ What are the circumstances?

- ❖ What is the relationship?

- ❖ ReCoVery – Let's get started to Rebuild.

- • Rebuild–

- • Rebuild together–

- • Rebuild in truth–

ReCoVery15

~ Prayer ~

ReCoVery

We can call on the Names of God Because our Father attests that
He is our Ever-Present Help. God is our All in All in every Challenge.
Below is a Name of God in Hebrew and the meaning.
We have access to call upon when in need.

Who is God to me Today...

Jehovah Shammah ~
The Lord Is There

ReCoVery

Romans Chapter 15

I have one request, dear friends: Pray for me. Pray strenuously with and for me—to God the Father, through the power of our Master Jesus, through the love of the Spirit—that I will be delivered from the lions' den of unbelievers in Judea. Pray also that my relief offering to the Jerusalem believers will be accepted in the spirit in which it is given. Then, God willing, I'll be on my way to you with a light and eager heart, looking forward to being refreshed by your company. God's peace be with all of you. Oh, yes!

—Romans 15:30–33 (MSG)

ReCoVery

Prayer is the catalysis that holds all of life together for the Christian lifestyle as well as the nonbeliever. They just don't believe that. Prayer transforms and changes things—situations, circumstances, and relationships. It is like the protein in the body. Protein is the catalysis that works as the building block of life. It helps the body build and repair every cell in the body. Its everyday purpose is to make better the life process of the body.

That is what prayer does. The daily engagement and purpose are to make better the life process of everybody, humanity. The true Word of God records that Christians are the salt of the earth and the light of the world. These verses expressed that the effectual prayer of a Christian transforms situations, circumstances, and relationships both in the earth and the world.

Why salt? Salt is a natural preservative. Why light? The natural process of light is to illuminate by removing darkness. Once becoming a Christian, we enter into the marvelous illuminating light of Jesus Christ, and we enter into the workings of life preservation with Jesus Christ for all of humanity.

Prayer is addressed and used much in the Bible, changing lives for the people that prayed. Prayer is a change agent for hope and justice. Jesus prayed before going to the cross, asking the Father if there were another way other than nailing Him to the cross to satisfy the sins of the world. And then he resolved the issues in obedience and stated, "Thy will be done in His life."

Jesus also prays to the Father for you and me. Our Father takes the stance that nothing—not life, death, troubles, distress, angelic powers, demonic powers, starvation, or mass weapons of control—will separate us from the love of Christ Jesus.

The enemy robs, kills, and destroys, but God has given us an abundance, more than enough, which is eternal life with Him. How can the enemy kill someone who has eternal life, to live forever? No kind of robbery, murder, or destruction can change eternal life. The Christian life is a win-win life forever! Our adversary does not want us to believe this fact. The adversary is so believably convincing with his lies of deception because he has the audacity to lie to you to your face. He doesn't hide. The adversary temptations are contingent on the border; rather you either know who you are in this life or you don't.

Can you think for yourself, or do you rely on others to think for you? The adversary asked Jesus if He were the Son of God. What if Jesus didn't know who He was? If He didn't know who He was, He knew where to get the answers to His problems. Jesus replied, "It is written." Our prayers are known before we pray them because God knows everything, but He desires that we commune and ask Him for what we need based on His word.

-*-Let's Reason Together -*-

Pray, my Abba Father. "David said, Oh You who hear prayer" (Psalm 65:2 NKJV).

> "So the helpless has hope, And unrighteousness must shut its mouth."
> —Job 5:16 (NASB 1977)

ReCoVery

We are to pray the Word of God for results. It is written for us to use it, read it, declare it, command it, and decree it. The Word of God reads that the adversary was more cunning than any other beast of the field when he deceived Eve in the garden of Eden. He is a superior deceiver of all the animals on the earth. Why engage in a conversation with a liar? Our conversation must be with Jesus Christ in prayer.

The book of Psalms is a book of prayers written predominantly by King David, changing his desperation into hope. The people of Nineveh, the story associated with Jonah, who was swallowed up by the big fish, prayed for forgiveness against destruction, and God resolved not to destroy them. Queen Ester prayed for her husband, King of Persia, Ahasuerus Xerxes, to rescue the people of her nation from destruction, and he did. King Jehoshaphat of Judah cried out to the Lord, asking for protection against multiple armies. King Jehoshaphat recited and attested to God that he did not know what to do, but his eyes were on God to hear his prayer in hope of saving his people from destruction. Hanna was a married woman without a child and prayed for a son. The Lord heard her request, and Hanna gave birth to a son, who became a prophet for the nation of Israel. Daniel was threatened and thrown into the lion's den for praying to God. Daniel didn't hide that he was praying three times a day and refused to stop praying to God. In addition, Daniel boldly opened his window, allowing all who were looking to see him pray to his God.

Prayer can be prayed for individual situations or situations of the earth and the world. We have the ordained right and authority as Christians to not only pray for our individual needs, but we can and should pray for needs on earth and needs in the world with expectations that our Father will hear and answer our requests. The prayer request is often good over evil. Our everyday struggle is good over evil. The plight of humanity is good over evil in our lives. The true Word of God reads that all things work together for good for those who are called. We rely on working together with God because it is the promise that we can expect Christ Jesus to help us with His ever-present character.

-*-Let's Reason Together -*-

Pray to learn to understand the importance of prayer. Prayer cannot be separated, divorced, or left out from your life!

- "I will declare the decree: the LORD hath said unto me ..." (Psalm 2:7–12 KJV)
- "You can command them all to ..." (Psalm 2:9 MSG)
- "Thou shalt also decree a thing, and it shall be established unto thee ..." (Job 22:28 KJV)

> "Why are you discouraged, my soul? Why are you so restless? Put your hope in God because I will still praise Him. He is my Savior and my God."
>
> —Psalm 43:5 (GW)

ReCoVery

Here is an individual situation that was bathed in prayer. My daughter, Leah Tabitha, did not receive her high school diploma on graduation day, and this fact just slipped our thoughts. Once getting accepted at her number-one college of choice, arriving on the day of registration, and moving into the dorms, Leah was informed that her high school diploma was a missing document. She would not be able to proceed with the registration process until the diploma was presented. We prayed. It was the weekend. We had driven over nine hours, and her high school was not only closed, but it was over fourteen hours away. Of course, we requested to speak with an administrator regarding this matter. Again, we were informed that this was the case. However, the administrator did allow us a leeway that if we could contact a high school official or teacher, someone to verify that Leah had indeed graduated from the named high school, that would be accepted. My daughter attended a private high school, and she informed us that teachers and office personnel often came into work on the weekends. We called the high school and left messages. Leah had several numbers of teachers who were called, but no one was answering that day. We made attempts to contact someone all day long, but all efforts failed. We decided to call it a draw and head back on our eight-hour drive. We were all sadly driving away but had not yet left the city limits when a call came from the college and stated that a teacher had called and verified Leah's attendance. If you get but one thing from these readings, please believe that our Lord Jesus Christ is forever faithful and with Him we can and will experience ReCoVery together from anything in this life.

The true Word of God reads that we do not always know what to pray for. Christ Himself intercedes on our behalf for the saints according to the will of the Father for our lives. Now, this is how all things work together. It works for our good because we have learned to love the Lord and we have accepted the call to purpose our lives for His use.

All of humanity is called, but not all will accept the calling. Christ stated that it is His desire that all of humanity would be saved and learn the knowledge of truth. It is Christ's desire that prayer is offered for all men. The question then is, "Who will pray for all men?" It is not a matter of knowing the individual, country, or nation. It is the instructions that we are to pray for those in authority to those who are in daily need, all men. Our new life of intercessions is to pray to our Father, expecting Him to listen and respond. Christ attests that he will reward those He sees openly and those who seek after Him with diligence. He expressed to Abram in the book of Genesis that He was His shield and exceedingly great reward. Jesus becomes our reward!

-*-Let's Reason Together -*-

Pray with purpose and listen with purpose. Sometimes it is of a prevailing and travailing effort. It is a two-way conversation of praying and listening.

> "I have one small request to make of you," she said. "I hope you won't turn me down …"
>
> —1 Kings 2:20 (TLB)

ReCoVery

While on several nursing travel assignments, I have often enjoyed and attended morning mass at the many large Catholic cathedrals in New York City before going to work. All are welcome to attend mass. I found this time with the Father in prayer—worshiping, singing, and taking communion—comforting in addition to my own personal time with the Lord in the morning before going to work. It is performed several times a day in a peacefully serene atmosphere.

The cathedrals are huge, but amazingly the serenity brings me into the bosom of Christ, especially when I arrive early and no one else is visibly seated in the pews. It feels like there is no other but me and God. The true Word of God reads that we are invited to symbolically engage in daily communion with the Father as often as we would like in remembrance of His death and return. When we do this, we have life. Christ is in us, and you are in Him. I have incorporated daily communion as a part of my daily prayer time with the Father. I deliberately purpose in my heart to remember His death for me and His return for me. The apostle Paul declares in the book of Acts to give oneself.

After we have experienced and recognized the need for ReCoVery, we realized that we are all recovering in this life from one thing or another. As we process our life challenges, feelings of loss after loss, hurt, pain, rejection, disappointments, unjust, and negative after negative, we are on the way to ReCoVery, a rebuilding.

Re ~ Rebuild … **Co** ~ Rebuild Together … **Very** ~ Rebuild in Truth

It is advantageous to rebuild with a new foundation. It is advantageous to rebuild with togetherness and like-minded individuals who have your best interest at heart and love you for you. It is advantageous to rebuild on nothing but the truth, so help "me," God. It is advantageous to pray to our Father Jesus Christ for assistance in everything because He cares for you!

~*~Let's Reason Together ~*~

We are to acquire a PhD in prayer by praying heaven down on our behalf!

> "The wicked man's fears will all come true and so will the good man's hopes."
> —Proverb 10:24 (TLB)

ReCoVery

Let's Reason in Our Thoughts for a Moment...God will perfect those things that concern you.

Are there any concerns understanding the importance to Pray to our Father Jesus Christ for assistance in everything because He cares for you!

❖ What is the situation?

❖ What are the circumstances?

❖ What is the relationship?

❖ ReCoVery ~ Let's get started to Rebuild.

• Rebuild~

• Rebuild together~

• Rebuild in truth~

ReCoVery 16

~ *Testimony* ~

ReCoVery

We can call on the Names of God Because our Father attests that He is our Ever-Present Help. God is our All in All in every Challenge. Below is a Name of God in Hebrew and the meaning. We have access to call upon when in need.

Who is God to me Today...

Jehovah Tsidkenu ~ The Lord Our Righteousness

ReCoVery

The LORD is my shepherd; I shall not want. He makes me to lie down in green pastures; He leads me beside the still waters. He restores my soul; He leads me in the paths of righteousness. For His name's sake. Yea, though I walk through the valley of the shadow of death, I will fear no evil; For You are with me; Your rod and Your staff, they comfort me. You prepare a table before me in the presence of my enemies; You anoint my head with oil; My cup runs over. Surely goodness and mercy shall follow me. All the days of my life; And I will dwell in the house of the LORD. Forever

—Psalm 23

The cross of Cavalry allowed me to take my King as my Shepherd. He takes away any wants that I may have. He granted me the most marvelous benefit of His care by making me lie down in His so lovely green pasture, which made me do right to myself even though I didn't know how to do right. He has led me into unspeakable joy by me saying "joy" (just one yes)! This yes allowed Him to come into my heart, and it gave me a stillness of His mind. I have a renewed mind. It is called the mind of Christ. His plan of ReCoVery was sealed and implemented for me at Cavalry. Cavalry predestined me for righteousness because right is right and right will always be right when it comes to right versus wrong. The blood-stain banner was Him as His blood dripped from His body, demonstrating the power of the name of Jesus. I have had challenges in the past and will be presented with challenges until His return. But the promise is that I'm not afraid because He will never leave me or forsake me. His tools of correction are designed to keep me in alignment with Him.

As we read earlier, every part of Scripture is God-breathed and useful one way or another, showing us truth, exposing our rebellion, correcting our mistakes, and training us to live God's way. Through the Word, we are put together and shaped up for the tasks God has for us. As I seek these truths, instructions, corrections, and training, they will result in my comfort. I will feel comforted by my Daddy, Abba, Lord Jesus Christ. It's all done publicly so He may be glorified and recognized by His enemies, which are also my enemies' sin, death, and hell. Thank You, Jesus. I'm anointed by Him to the overflow of having Him His goodness, and His mercy all the days of my life, which is forever in Christ Jesus.

-*-Let's Reason Together -*-

"Surely goodness and mercy shall follow me. All the days of my life."

ReCoVery

Jesus was the blood-stain banner that waved the announcement, "It is Finished" (John 19:30). Christ's blood-stain announcement made me free, and the price was paid. Now I have eternal life. Eternal life is the most important thing that the enemy desired to steal from us in the attempt to prevent us from living in paradise with the Father. The enemy's plans for my life were for me to continue to assist him in my own self-destruction of flesh and soul, hoping I would kill myself and I would die and go to hell with him. But God, my King Jesus Christ, has allowed me to overcome the enemy by the blood of the Lamb, the words of my testimony, and I didn't love my life so much that I refused to give it up. Therefore, I can rejoice by having joy (just one yes) to the gospel of Jesus Christ, the good news.

I was born in Columbia, South Carolina. My parents separated when I was promoted to the third grade. I grew up in Brooklyn, New York, in a low-income family with my mother, father, and two siblings. But there were times when my parents were separated from each other due to domestic issues, but they would always get back together. My mother finally decided one day to separate from my father because he was an alcoholic, physical abuser, and adulterer. We relocated to New York City. I remained in New York until my adulthood. When my mother moved to New York City, we lived with my mother's brother on Herkimer Street between Rockaway Avenue and Saratoga Avenue.

My mother worked several jobs and received additional assistance from the Department of Welfare. My family and I lived in several ghetto communities in Brooklyn, Bedford Stuyvesant, Brownsville, and East New York, all of which I greatly disliked. As a little girl growing up in South Carolina, I enjoyed walking barefoot, climbing trees, and visiting neighbors who cared about my safety and well-being. I didn't like the dirtiness, no-grass, unsafe feeling walking through the long, dark hallway up to our second-floor tenement apartment building. Thank God we lived on the front side of the building, and I would often call at my brother's bedroom window from the street in hope that he would be home and come down to escort me through the jungle.

My playground area was on dangerous rooftops, jumping from one apartment roof to another and running through unsafe apartment alleyways from one building to the next and filthy cement backyards where people threw their garbage out the windows. As a child, I remembered the moment I vowed to myself that my children would never live like that. New York City was ugly, cruel, and cold to me as a child. I also vowed that my children would never see their mother drunk and out of control. Christ Jesus heard that prayer request, and He honored my heart's desire like a loving Father.

-*-Let's Reason Together -*-
_____

"And I shall dwell in the house of The LORD."

ReCoVery

The subway was something to be reckoned with—the continuous movement of the train, unsafe danger of walking in between cars, the unfriendly people never saying anything during the ride to your destination, and the dark, damp, and creepy subway stops. But as adoptable beings, we learn to accept, adjust, and keep it moving (KIM). Life was not good. I lived in drug-infested neighborhoods.

My brother, who was my dear saving grace, decided to leave the family, get married, and enter the military, the Marines. He was both a father and a brother. The time era was the late 1960s/early 1970s. The drugs in the inner city took the lives of the young and old. The police department would advertise on television, inviting the public to call the number on the television screen, offering a reward to anyone who would report drug dealings in the neighborhood.

I so desperately wanted to call and report my neighbors, but I was afraid it could possibly hurt my sister and brother because those same people were our friends. If they were to get busted, my siblings could be visiting someone during the bust. Every afternoon there were after-school movies on television about children on alcohol and drugs, predominately heroin, starting from elementary school on up. I was so afraid of becoming addicted that I never thought I would be one of them. Both of my parents and brother are deceased.

I'm grateful for my rebirth into the kingdom of Jesus Christ. Jesus Christ did a new thing in my life, and I received it. He has given me a God-given good life, and I'm thankful. Thanksgiving is my favorite holiday because I will forever have much to be thankful for in this life. I have been given a platform of ministries, sound mind, good health, and lovely, healthy, drug-free children, Larry Randal Jr., Yuri Stefon, and Leah Tabitha. I love my children, and I especially love to hear them call me "Mommy!" The sound of "Mommy" just melts my heart.

I have sought the career of a professional registered nurse, and I have been blessed by my career of choice versus my drug of choice. Christianity has given me a good life, great Christian friends, and superb Christian leadership. I accepted my Lord and Savior Jesus Christ while attending the Brooklyn Tabernacle Church in Brooklyn, New York. When I accepted Christ, I was so afraid of losing my sobriety that I ran to church for safekeeping. I would attend Tuesday night prayer at the church directly after work. I would arrive early, waiting for the church doors to open. I hoped and prayed that I would stay sober because I was frightened that my Christian born-again experience would fade away.

I had tried to be sober before, and it faded away shortly after. Our King has kept me, and the same life-changing power can keep you too! In addition, the Father changed my birth name from Dorothy Hoytette Bowser to Joy-Michael Bowser. There was a time in my life when I needed the joy of the Lord to be my strength, and Lord was. I also felt like I needed supernatural strength in order to stay alive, and He gave me the strength liken unto the archangel Michael, hence, Joy-Michael.

-*-Let's Reason Together -*-
_____

Forever … Amen.

ReCoVery

The Lord Reveals His Omnipotence to Job (38:1–41 NKJV)

Then the Lord answered Job out of the whirlwind, and said:

"Who is this who darkens counsel By words without knowledge? Now prepare yourself like a man; I will question you, and you shall answer Me.

Where were you when I laid the foundations of the earth? Tell Me, if you have understanding. Who determined its measurements? Surely you know! Or who stretched the line upon it? To what were its foundations fastened? Or who laid its cornerstone, When the morning stars sang together, And all the sons of God shouted for joy? Or who shut in the sea with doors, When it burst forth and issued from the womb; When I made the clouds its garment, And thick darkness its swaddling band;

When I fixed My limit for it, And set bars and doors; When I said, 'This far you may come, but no farther, And here your proud waves must stop!' Have you commanded the morning since your days began, And caused the dawn to know its place, That it might take hold of the ends of the earth, And the wicked be shaken out of it? It takes on form like clay under a seal, And stands out like a garment. From the wicked their light is withheld, And the upraised arm is broken. Have you entered the springs of the sea? Or have you walked in search of the depths? Have the gates of death been revealed to you? Or have you seen the doors of the shadow of death? Have you comprehended the breadth of the earth? Tell Me, if you know all this. Where is the way to the dwelling of light? And darkness, where is its place, That you may take it to its territory, That you may know the paths to its home? Do you know it, because you were born then, Or because the number of your days is great? Have you entered the treasury of snow, Or have you seen the treasury of hail, Which I have reserved for the time of trouble, For the day of battle and war? By what way is light diffused, Or the east wind scattered over the earth? Who has divided a channel for the overflowing water, Or a path for the thunderbolt, To cause it to rain on a land where there is no one, A wilderness in which there is no man; To satisfy the desolate waste, And cause to spring forth the growth of tender grass? Has the rain a father? Or who has begotten the drops of dew? From whose womb comes the ice? And the frost of heaven, who gives it birth? The waters harden like stone, And the surface of the deep is frozen. Can you bind the cluster of he Pleiades, Or loose the belt of Orion? Can you bring out Mazzaroth in its season? Or can you guide the Great Bear with its cubs? Do you know the ordinances of the heavens? Can you set their dominion over the earth? Can you lift up your voice to the clouds, That an abundance of water may cover you? Can you send out lightnings, that they may go, And say to you, 'Here we are!'? Who has put wisdom in the mind? Or who has given understanding to the heart? Who can number the clouds by wisdom? Or who can pour out the bottles of heaven, When the dust hardens in clumps, And the clods cling together? Can you hunt the prey for the lion, Or satisfy the appetite of the young lions, When they crouch in their dens, Or lurk in their lairs to lie in wait? Who provides food for the raven, When its young ones cry to God, And wander about for lack of food?"

Part Five

~ Forever ~

Tools For ReCoVery Walk with Me and Work My Tools

ReCoVery

Tools for ReCoVery
Walk with Me and Work My Tools

Anyone born into the family of God is allowed access to the kingdom of God. If you are without a family - father, and mother in love with you, today, we are willing to become your family.

- "When my father and my mother forsake me, Then the LORD will take care of me." (Psalm 27:10 NKJV)
- "For through the living and eternal word of God you have been Born Again as the Children of a parent who is immortal (the ability to live forever eternal life), not of mortal/human life." (1 Peter 1:23 GNT)
- "All wrongdoing is sin … We know [with confidence] that anyone born of God does not habitually sin; but He [Jesus] who was born of God [carefully] keeps and protects him, and the evil one does not touch him." (1 John 5:17–18 AMP)

Jesus Christ

- "For this purpose the Son of God was manifested, that He might Destroy the works of the devil." (1 John 3:8 KJV)

The Name of Jesus

- "Most assuredly, I say to you, he who believes in Me, the works that I do he will do also; and greater works than these he will do, because I go to My Father. And whatever you ask in My name, that I will do, that the Father may be glorified in the Son. If you ask anything in My name, I will do it." (John 14:12–14 NKJV)
- "Holy Father protect them by the power of your name, the name you gave me, so that they may be one as we are one. While I was with them, I protected them and kept them safe by that name you gave me." (John 17:12 NIV)

The Word

- "For the Word that God speaks is alive and full of power [making it active, operative, energizing, and effective]; it is sharper than any two-edged sword, penetrating to the dividing line of the breath of life (soul) and [the immortal] spirit, and of joints and marrow [of the deepest parts of our nature], exposing and sifting and analyzing and judging the very thoughts and purposes of the heart." (Hebrews 4:12 AMPC)
- "My people are destroyed for lack of knowledge …" (Hosea 4:6 AMPC)
  This lack of knowledge is the lack of studying the Word of God.

ReCoVery

Tools for ReCoVery
Walk with Me and Work My Tools

Holy Spirit

- "The Helper whom the Father will send in my name {Jesus}, will teach you everything and make you remember." (John 14:26 GNT)
- "The Holy Spirit will come on you and give you POWER … to be my witnesses. You will tell people everywhere about me … in every part of the world." (Acts 1:8 ERV)

Prayer and Fasting

- "This kind does not go out except by prayer and fasting." (Matthew 17:21 NKJ)

Love

- "God is Love." (1 John 4:16 TLB)

Prayer

- Pray for Angelic Protection: Jesus said, don't you realize that I am able right now to call to my Father and twelve companies (72,000 or more) —more, if I want them—of fighting angels would be here, battle-ready? Matthew 26:53 MSG. Isaiah 37:36 MSG, stated that one angel alone killed 185,000 men.

Praise

- "You have taught the little children to praise you perfectly. May their example shame and silence your enemies!" (Psalm 8:2 TLB)

The Blood of the Lamb/Your Testimony

- "And they [Believers] overcame him/Adversary by the blood of the Lamb." (Revelation 12:11 KJV)

Be Transformed into a New Life

- "Do not conform yourselves to the standards of this world, but let God transform you inwardly by a complete change of your mind …" (Romans 12:2 GNT)

ReCoVery

Tools for ReCoVery
Walk with Me and Work My Tools

Submit to God

- "Submit (accept or undergo, often unwillingly) yourselves therefore to God. Resist the devil, and he will flee from you." (James 4:7 KJV)

Resist the Devil

- "Submit yourselves therefore to God. Resist (A refusal to comply with or accept something) the devil, and he will flee from you." (James 4:7 KJV)

ReCoVery

Tools for ReCoVery
Walk with Me and Work My Tools

Faith

- "But without faith it is impossible to please him: for he that cometh to God must believe that he is, and that he is a rewarder of them that diligently seek him." (Hebrews 11:6 KJV)

Obedience

- "How does a child show their parents that they love them? Obedience is the only way. "If you love me, obey me." (John 4:15 TLB)
- "To obey is better than sacrifice and to heed is better …" (1 Samuel 15:22 KJV)
- "I am in My Father, and you in Me, and I in you. He who has My commandments and keeps them, it is he who loves Me. And he who loves Me will be loved by My Father, and I will love him and manifest Myself to him." (John 14:20–21)

The Word of God states that faith is the substance of things hoped for and the evidence of things not seen. And without faith, it is impossible to please God. So having faith pleases God, and we only need a mustard seed-size of faith. Faith is often interconnected with obedience. There are much more benefits when the two are united, faith in His word and obedience in His word. The Word assures us that Jesus will manifest Himself in us in our obedience. John 14:23 (NKJV) reads, "Jesus answered and said to him, If anyone loves Me, he will keep My word; and My Father will love him, and We will come to him and make Our home with him."

In addition, verse 26 tells us that Jesus will send the Holy Spirit to teach us all things from the word of God and help us memorize all things from the word of God. In our obedience, we now have the Father, Son, and Holy Spirit indwelling and assisting us in this life every step of the way.

1 Samuel 15:22 reads, "that it is better to obey the voice of the Lord than to sacrifice." This is important because Christ has already died and resurrected as the sacrificial lamb. The Lord is delighted when we listen and act on what He has told us to do in faith. The act of disobedience makes again a sacrifice, and your sacrifice will never be better than following God's instructions, making your sacrificial choice without God, and resulting in unpleasing results without faith.

Many times, we are the sacrifice of our own disbelief and doubt. Both are precipitated by fear. I believe that the opposite of faith is fear. God assures us that the spirit of fear does not come from Him. 2 Timothy 1:7 (NKJV) reads, "For God hath not given us the spirit of fear; but of power, and of love, and of a sound mind." Therefore, we can trust that we have all that we need to make a faith-based decision in obedience.

ReCoVery
Tools for ReCoVery
Walk with Me and Work My Tools

The Whole Armor of God

So put on God's armor now! Then when the evil day comes, you will be able to resist the enemy's attacks, and after fighting to the end, you will still hold your ground. So stand ready, with truth as a belt tight around your waist, righteousness as your breastplate, and your shoes the readiness to announce the good news of peace. At all times, carry faith as a shield, for with it you will be able to put out all the burning arrows shot by the evil one. And accept salvation as a helmet and the word of God as the sword the Spirit gives you. Do all this in prayer, asking for God's help. Pray on every occasion, as the Spirit leads (Ephesians 6:10–20).

Truth

- "And ye shall know the truth, and the truth shall make you free." (John 8:32 KJV)

Breastplate of Righteousness

- "Or, you may fall on your knees and pray—to God's delight! You'll see God's smile and celebrate, finding yourself set right with God. You'll sing God's praises to everyone you meet, testifying, 'I messed up my life—and let me tell you, it wasn't worth it. But God stepped in and saved me from certain death. I'm alive again! Once more I see the light!' (Job 33:26–28 MSG)
- "But the righteous man shall live by faith!" (Romans 1:16–17 NKJV)

Your Shoes

- "Put on your shoes so that you are ready to spread the Good News that gives peace. Be anxious for nothing, but in everything by prayer and supplication, with thanksgiving, let your requests be made known to God; and the peace of God, which surpasses all understanding, will guard your hearts and minds through Christ Jesus." (Philippians 4:6–7 NKJV)

Shield of Faith

- "How then shall they call on Him in whom they have not believed? And how shall they believe in Him of whom they have not heard? And how shall they hear without a preacher? And how shall they preach unless they are sent? As it is written: How beautiful are the feet of those who preach the gospel of peace, who bring glad tidings of good things! But they have not all obeyed the gospel. For Isaiah says, "Lord, who has believed our report? So, then faith comes by hearing, and hearing by the word of God." (Romans 10:14–17 NKJV)

ReCoVery

Tools for ReCoVery
Walk with Me and Work My Tools

Helmet of Salvation

- "It's crucial that we keep a firm grip on what we've heard so that we don't drift off. If the old message delivered by the angels was valid and nobody got away with anything, do you think we can risk neglecting this latest message, this magnificent salvation? First of all, it was delivered in person by the Master, then accurately passed on to us by those who heard it from him. All the while God was validating it with gifts through the Holy Spirit, all sorts of signs and miracles, as he saw fit." (Hebrews 2:1–4 MSG)

The Sword of the Spirit

- "The sword of the spirit is the word of God. The word of God is alive and active, sharper than any double-edged sword. It cuts all the way through, to where the soul and spirit meets, to where joints and marrow come together. It judges the desires and thoughts of the heart. There is nothing that can be hid from God; everything in all creation is exposed and lies open before his eyes. And it is to him that we must all give an account of ourselves." (Hebrews 4:12–13 GNT)

Prayer

- "Don't fret or worry. Instead of worrying, pray. Let petitions and praises shape your worries into prayers, letting God know your concerns. Before you know it, a sense of God's wholeness, everything coming together for good, will come and settle you down. It's wonderful what happens when Christ displaces worry at the center of your life." (Philippians 4:7 MSG)

Believe Me

- "I am in my Father and my Father is in me. If you can't believe that believe what you see—these works. The person who trusts me will not only do what I'm doing but even greater things, because I am, on my way to the Father, giving you the same work to do that I've been doing. You can count on it. From now on, whatever you request along the lines of who I am and what I am doing, I'll do it. That's how the Father will be seen for who he is in the Son. Whatever you request in this way, I'll do." (John 14:11–14 MSG)

You Shall Love the Lord Your God

- "You shall love the Lord your God with all your heart, with all your soul, with all your strength, and with all your mind, and your neighbor as yourself." (Luke 10:27 NKJV)

ReCoVery
Tools for ReCoVery
Walk with Me and Work My Tools

The Supernatural Trinity

Our God has made supernatural provisions for His followers/disciples to empower them with gifts designed to equip them to grow and develop their supernatural abilities for the use of kingdom work in everyday life on earth as it is in heaven. If we choose to invest in our God-given treasures by making the commitment to do His work - He will not leave us or forsake us. These God-designed supernatural gifts are for you and me, and they have miraculous undertakings (a formal pledge or promise by God to do something).

Supernatural Trinity

The most amazing, beautiful, and life-sustaining gifts that parents provide for their children are love, guidance, and protection. Our Father in heaven has gifted us with this unique and supernatural wonderment in his Trinity that lives in us: the Father, the Son, and the Holy Spirit.

The Father

- "And what agreement has the temple of God with idols? For you are the temple of the living God. As God has said: 'I will dwell in them and walk among them. I will be their God, and they shall be My people.'" (2 Corinthians 6:16 NKJV)

The Son

- "To them God willed to make known what are the riches of the glory of this mystery among the Gentiles: which is Christ in you, the hope of glory." (Colossians 1:27 NKJV)

The Holy Spirit

- "Our Savior Jesus Christ, who has abolished death and brought life and immortality to the light through the gospel ... nevertheless I am not ashamed, for I know whom I have believed and am persuaded that He is able to keep what I have committed to Him until that Day. Hold fast the pattern of sound words which you have heard from me, in faith and love which are in Christ Jesus. That good thing, which was committed to you, keep by the Holy Spirit who dwells in us." (2 Timothy 1:12–14 NKJV)

ReCoVery

Tools for ReCoVery
Walk with Me and Work My Tools

Supernatural Everlasting Presences: He Will Be with Us Until the End of the Age

- "And Jesus came and spoke to them, saying: 'All authority has been given to Me in heaven and on earth. Go therefore and make disciples of all the nations, baptizing them in the name of the Father and of the Son and of the Holy Spirit, teaching them to observe all things that I have commanded you; and lo, I am with you always, even to the end of the age.'" (Matthew 28:18–20 NKJV)

Supernatural Agent

- "Peter answered them, 'All of you must turn to God and change the way you think and act, and each of you must be baptized in the name of Jesus Christ so that your sins will be forgiven. Then you will receive the Holy Spirit as a gift. This promise belongs to you and to your children and to everyone who is far away. It belongs to everyone who worships the Lord our God.'" (Acts 2:38–39 GWT)

Supernatural Guide

- "But when He, the Spirit of truth, comes, He will guide you into all the truth; for He will not speak on His own initiative, but whatever He hears, He will speak; and He will disclose to you what is to come." (John 16:13 NKJV)

Supernatural Teacher

- "But the Helper, the Holy Spirit, whom the Father will send in My name, He will teach you all things, and bring to your remembrance all that I said to you." (John 14:26 NKJV)
- "But you have received the Holy Spirit, and he lives within you, in your hearts, so that you don't need anyone to teach you what is right. For he teaches you all things, and he is the Truth, and no liar; and so, just as he has said, you must live in Christ, never to depart from him." (1 John 2:27 TLB)

Supernatural Comforter

- "If you love me, obey me; and I will ask the Father and he will give you another Comforter and he will never leave you." (John 14:15–16 TLB)
- "But I will send you the Comforter—the Holy Spirit, the source of all truth. He will come to you from the Father and will tell you all about me." (John 15:26 TLB)

ReCoVery

Tools for ReCoVery
Walk with Me and Work My Tools

Supernatural Communications

- "I will explain why. Those who have the gift of speaking in a different language are not speaking to people. They are speaking to God. No one understands them—they are speaking secret things through the Spirit." (1 Corinthians 14:2 ERV)
- "When they arrest you and hand you over, do not worry beforehand about what you are to say, but say whatever is given you in that hour; for it is not you who speak, but it is the Holy Spirit." (Matthew 10:19 NKJV)
- "Praying always with all prayer and supplication in the Spirit, being watchful to this end with all perseverance and supplication for all the saints (followers/disciples)." (Ephesians 6:18 NKJV)
- "Most assuredly, I say to you, he who believes in Me, the works that I do he will do also; and greater works than these he will do, because I go to My Father. And whatever you ask in My name, that I will do, that the Father may be glorified in the Son. If you ask anything in My name, I will do it." (John 14:12–14 NKJV)
- "And these signs will follow those who believe: In My name they will cast out demons; they will speak with new tongues; they will take up serpents; and if they drink anything deadly, it will by no means hurt them; they will lay hands on the sick, and they will recover." (Mark 16:17–18 NKJV)

ReCoVery

The Joy of ReCoVery

"The **law** (principles/rules) of the LORD is **perfect** (complete/mature) refreshing the soul."

"The **statutes** (law enacted by a legislative body of a government) of the LORD are **trustworthy** (honest) making wise the simple."

"The **precepts** (conduct) of the LORD are **right** (good) giving joy to the heart."

"The **commands** (authority) of the LORD are **radiant** (bright with joy and hope) giving light to the eyes."

"The **fear** (respect) of the LORD is **pure** (free) enduring forever."

"The **decrees** (eternal purposes) of the LORD are **firm** (secure) and all of them are righteous.'

—Psalm 19:7–10 (NIV)

ReCoVery

My Affirmation Decision

I desire a personal Born-Again Relationship and Life with JESUS CHRIST. Father, I know I am a sinner. I invite you to live in my heart. I will confess Romans 10:8-10 Living Bible (TLB).

MY NEW LIFE BEGINS HERE!

8 – "For salvation that comes from trusting Christ which is what we preach is already within easy reach of each of us; in fact, it is as near as our own hearts and mouths."

9 – "For if you tell others with your own mouth that Jesus Christ is your Lord and believe in your own heart that God has raised him from the dead, you (I) will be saved."

10 – "For it is by believing in his heart that a man becomes right with God; and with his mouth he tells others of his faith, confirming his salvation."

Name: _____ IS JESUS AMAZING DISCIPLE

Date: _____ BORN AGAIN BIRTHDAY

ReCoVery

"And Asa cried out to the LORD his God, and said, "LORD, it is nothing for You to help, whether with many or with those who have no power
help us!
O LORD our God, for we rest on You, and in Your Name, we go against this multitude. O LORD You are our God; do not let man prevail against You!"

—2 Chronicles 14:11 (NKJV)

ReCoVery
References

Introduction

1   "Outbreak 10 of the Worst Pandemics in History 2020," MPHonline, accessed November 18, 2020, https://www.mphonline.org/worst-pandemics-in-history/.

2   "Matthew Henry's Commentary John 17," BibleGateway, accessed November 18, 2020, https://www.biblegateway.com/resources/matthew-henry/John.17.20-John.17.23.

Chapter 1

3   Kimberly A. Whitler, "Why Word of Mouth Marketing Is The Most Important Social Media," *Forbes Online*, accessed October 1, 2018, https://www.forbes.com/sites/kimberlywhitler/2014/07/17/why-word-of-mouth marketing-is-the-most-important-social-media/?sh=42a6428654a8.

Chapter 2

4   "By Discovery Mood &Anxiety Program Mental Health Treatment, Drugs of Abuse: What's the Difference Between Meth, Heroin, and Xanax?" https://discoverymood.com/blog/drugs-abuse-whats-difference-meth-heroin-xanax/.

5   Types of mental health issues and illnesses 2021, Better Health Channel, accessed January 17, 2022, https://www.betterhealth.vic.gov.au/health/servicesandsupport/types-of-mental-health-issues-and-illnesses.

Chapter 4

6   "Laws Criminalizing Apostasy," Library of Congress, last modified December 30, 2020, https://www.loc.gov/law/help/apostasy/.

Chapter 5

7   Shreya Dasgupta, "Can any Animal talk and use Language like Humans?", accessed October 13, 2020, http://www.bbc.com/earth/story/20150216-can-any-animals-talk-like-humans.

Chapter 13

8   Sarah Ryley and Pete Donohue, "Exclusive: Safest and Riskiest areas of New York's Subway System Reveal in Daily News Investigation," *New York Daily News*, accessed December 3, 2020, https://www.nydailynews.com/new-york/nyc-crime/daily-news-analysis-reveals-crime-rankings-city-subway-system-article-1.1836918.

Chapter 14

9   Thu-Huong Ha, "'No man is an island' the infamous quotation by John Donne 17th century British Poet. John Donne's Solemn 400-year-old Poem Against Isolationism is Resonating Today Quartz Discovery Online," accessed November 3, 2020, https://qz.com/716088/john-donnes-solemn-400-year-old-poem-against-isolationism-is-resonating-with-brits-today.

Printed in the United States
by Baker & Taylor Publisher Services